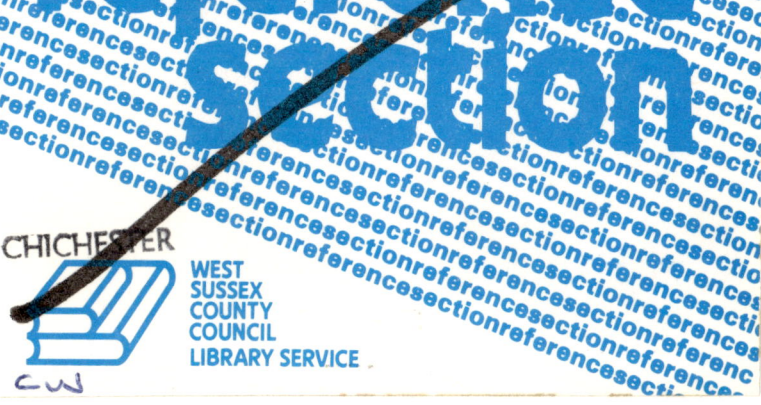

Naval and Marine Badges and Insignia of World War 2

By the same author

Army Badges and Insignia of World War 2: Book 1
Army Badges and Insignia of World War 2: Book 2
Army Badges and Insignia since 1945: Book 1
Ribbons of Orders, Decorations and Medals
Air Force Badges and Insignia of World War 2

Guido Rosignoli

Naval and Marine Badges and Insignia of World War 2

Great Britain, U.S.S.R., Denmark, Germany, France, Italy, U.S.A., Japan, Poland, Netherlands, Finland

BLANDFORD PRESS
Poole   Dorset

First published in the U.K. in 1980

*Copyright © 1980 Blandford Press Ltd,
Link House, West Street,
Poole, Dorset, BH15 1LL*

ISBN 0 7137 0919 7

All rights reserved. No part of this book may be reproduced or transmitted in any form or by any means, electronic or mechanical, including photocopying, recording or any information storage and retrieval system, without permission in writing from the Publisher.

WEST SUSSEX LIBRARIES

Copy No. E105881	Class No. 359.14		
Supplier MACAULAY	Date Invoiced 26. SEP. 1980		
1st Loc. CWR	Initials FW	2nd Loc.	Initials
3rd Loc.	Initials	4th Loc.	Initials

REFERENCE

*Set in V-I-P Plantin 9/10pt
Set, printed and bound in Great Britain by
Fakenham Press Limited,
Fakenham, Norfolk*

Contents

Introduction	7
Acknowledgements	9
Great Britain (*Plates 1–11*)	11
The Colour Plates	13
The Black and White Plates	77
U.S.S.R. (*Plates 11–14*)	103
Denmark (*Plates 15–17*)	107
Germany (*Plates 18–27*)	110
France (*Plates 28–32*)	120
Italy (*Plates 33–39*)	125
U.S.A. (*Plates 40–52*)	134
Japan (*Plates 53–58*)	152
Poland (*Plates 59–62*)	156
Netherlands (*Plates 63–66*)	160
Finland (*Plates 67–70*)	164

Introduction

The sacrifices and sufferings encountered in the course of space exploration cannot be compared with those endured by humanity in exploring its own planet.

Man's inquisitive mind wanted to learn what lay across the river, across the lake and then across the sea. Flimsy little boats sailed the oceans at a time when sailors still believed that their ship could topple over the edge of the Earth at any moment.

When nations organised expeditions to conquer new lands, empires were born and, to defend and to enlarge them, fleets were created, battling against each other for centuries in faraway seas. World War 2, in which conventional ships fought each other with sophisticated but still conventional weapons, was the last episode of this struggle.

Naval uniforms and insignia did not evolve in the same manner as those of the army and, later, modern developments led to a rather austere uniformity. Sailors were not counted by the regiment on the battlefield and therefore did not need to wear colourful clothing, nor, later, did they need camouflage in the battlefield's background. Thus they retained their traditional dress.

The handling of ships was based on team work—hard work—which called for practicality of dress; distinguishing badges were not required until the idea was adopted of assigning men to specific tasks and a class of specialists appeared and eventually developed in accordance with modern technology.

However, the apparent navy blue uniformity of this book's illustrations should not lead the reader to minimise the subject, as in fact 'naval insignia' is the most difficult one I have ever encountered and one of the most fascinating.

The long predominance of Britain on the seas led the Royal Navy to become the catalyst for all naval standards but, although other navies followed these standards, basically they retained their own traditions and customs, which were displayed as details of dress. The gunners, for instance, were usually identified by crossed cannons but the badge differed from one navy to another and had a different meaning, as often it showed qualification and rate contemporaneously.

All navies unified under the same symbol, the foul anchor, but, even in this case, the expert collector could distinguish the nationality of a specific badge.

The designation of naval officers' ranks followed two patterns: the British pattern, with standard titles from Captain to Sub-Lieutenant, or the

Continental system of referring the ranks to a specific type of ship, as used for example in France, Germany and Italy. These ranks have been described in the original language to avoid any confusion.

Any available information, including brief historical introductions, has been gathered together in this volume which I hope will be of some use to my readers.

G. Rosignoli,
Farnham, Surrey.

Acknowledgments

I would like to thank:

Miss Ursula Stuart Mason, Head of Public Relations and Mr J. Mundy, Keeper of the Department of Weapons and Antiquities, of the National Maritime Museum; Mr Stan A. Statham, Lieutenant Hugh F. Wolfensohn, R.N. and Major A. G. Brown, M.B.E., R.M.

Captain 3rd Rank A. Goroziy, Assistant Naval Attaché at the Soviet Embassy in London and Mr M. Fateev, Head Keeper of the Naval War Museum at Leningrad.

Mrs Inga Fl. Rasmussen, Curator of the Tøjhusmuseet, Copenhagen.

Dr Freidrich Herrmann.

Mr Bernard Jamin.

Geom. Licio Granata.

Commander James H. Cromwell, J.A.G.C., U.S.N. and Y.N.I. W. J. Tilton, U.S.N., Public Affairs Officer of U.S.S., Holland.

Mr K. Barbarski and the Polish Institute and Sikorski Museum.

Captain H. Ringoir, Hon. Gunner of the R.N.A., Commander F.C. van Oosten, R.N.N.(Rtd), director of Naval History at the Historical Department of the Naval Staff.

Mr Markku Melkko, Director of the Sotamuseo, at Helsinki.

The Prince Consort Library, Aldershot.

My most sincere thanks to my wife Diana for her assistance.

To
Inga Fl. Rasmussen

Great Britain

The Royal Navy

The Royal Navy traces the origins of its power to Elizabethan times, when the period of great expansion started, as Britain could expand only across the seas. In later years, the Royal Navy, its organisation and uniforms set a pattern that was followed by other nations all over the world.

The first uniform regulations were issued by Lord Anson's Board of Admiralty in 1748 in order to set a distinction between naval and other officers, as well as from the need to lay down more precise rules of rank and predence among naval officers themselves.

The seamen were issued with simple garments, the cost of which was deducted from their wages; the navy bought these clothes from a slop seller and ship's commanders occasionally tried to improve the appearance of their own men. In 1757, the Navy Board set up its own Slop Office, which, in 1827, became a responsibility of the Victualling Board and, 5 years later, of the Controller of Victualling under the Admiralty.

Meanwhile, new orders and regulations continued to modify the officers' dress. Regulations published in 1825 sanctioned the use of a blue cloth cap and of a round jacket and, when coats were ordered to be worn buttoned up, the elaborate lapels were discarded. Pantaloons or trousers replaced the white breeches and, finally, blue trousers were adopted in 1856.

Distinction lace on the sleeves of flag officers was introduced in 1783 and was extended to the other officers in 1856, with the addition of the curl in the uppermost row of lace for officers of the executive branch only. Non-executive officers, i.e. of the 'civil' branches, wore different uniforms until 1890: rank stripes without curl but with the addition of coloured velvet, later cloth, in between the stripes from 1864. In January 1915, the use of the curl was extended to engineer officers and, in 1918, to the other branches.

In 1919, the flag officers' narrow stripe was reduced from $\frac{5}{8}$ in (15.9 mm) to $\frac{1}{2}$ in (12.7 mm) in width and the order stated that the modification had obtained the King's approval, but in fact His Majesty had not been consulted at all. He, therefore, ignored the new rule and members of the Royal Family have continued to wear the old stripes on naval uniform to the present day. The $\frac{1}{2}$ in (12.7 mm) gold lace stripe was replaced by a larger stripe, $\frac{9}{16}$ in (14 mm) in width, in 1931.

The officers' uniform regulations were first published in book form, with plates of illustrations, on 1 January 1825 and later editions were issued in 1879, 1891, 1924 and 1937.

Plate 1. Cap and Other Insignia

The officers' cap was made of navy blue cloth, fitted with peak, chin strap and a black mohair band $1\frac{3}{4}$ in (44.5 mm) in width.

The cap badge consisted of a wreath of gold laurel leaves surrounding a silver foul anchor with the Royal Crown above embroidered in gold and silver; the whole anchor could be either embroidered in silver or partly made of silver metal.

This badge was adopted in 1856 in two versions: as above, embroidered in gold and silver for executive officers or in gold for officers of the civil branches. From about 1870 to 1891 the cap badge was usually embellished by a gold ring around the anchor; earlier badges were considerably smaller than those prescribed in the 1937 Uniform Regulations, which were $2\frac{9}{16}$ in (65 mm) high by $3\frac{5}{16}$ in (85 mm) broad.

By the end of World War I all naval officers wore the same type of cap badge but later, in 1940, the chaplains obtained a new badge with the crown and anchor in gold and silver as usual and the laurel wreath embroidered in black silk, veined with gold wire. A khaki cap with a bronze badge could be worn with khaki uniform when exposed to enemy fire.

The chin strap was made of black patent calf leather, the peak of the cap of senior ranks entitled to embroidery was covered with blue cloth and bound with leather and that of all the other officers was made of plain black leather.

The embroidery for flag officers and the Commodore 1st Class depicted gold oak leaves in two rows, each $\frac{3}{4}$ in (19 mm) wide, while the Commodore 2nd Class, Captain and Commander had only one row of gold oak leaves embroidered along the front edge of the peak.

The embroidery was introduced in the mid-nineteenth century, originally in the form of a gold stripe, which became oak leaves, for executive officers only, in 1860. The use of oak leaves was extended to engineer officers in 1915 and to all branches in 1918.

The Admiral of the Fleet, Vice-Admiral and Rear-Admiral of the United Kingdom, Aide-de-Camp to the King, Honorary Physician and Surgeon to the King and Naval Equerries to the King or to members of the Royal Family wore the Royal Cypher in dull silver on the plaited shoulder cords of the aiguillette, on the epaulettes, or on the shoulder straps. The officers of flag rank had the cypher below the crown, the others had it superimposed upon the lowest row of gold lace, the bottom of the cypher being even with the lower edge of the stripe.

The Personal Aide-de-Camp to the King wore a special cypher with block letters, each $\frac{11}{16}$ in (17.5 mm) in height. In the case of both devices, when more than one Royal Cypher was worn, the actual cyphers were smaller as, in specific cases, an officer who had held an appointment under more than

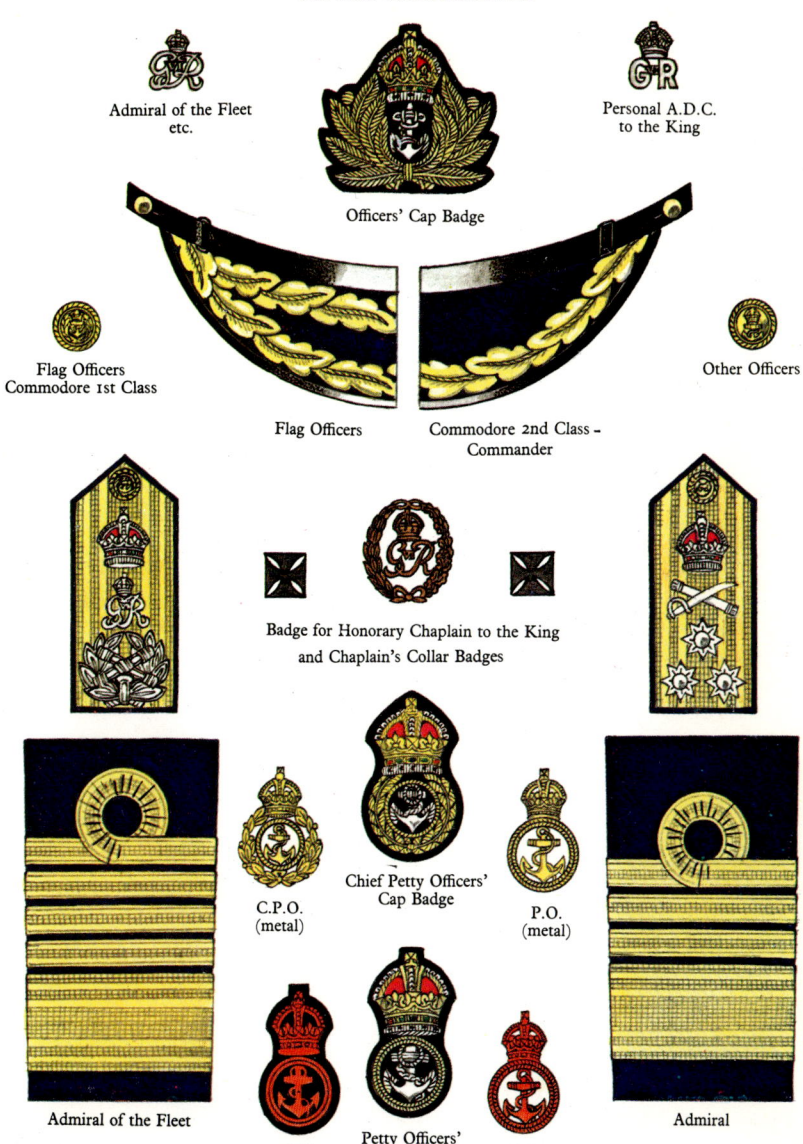

GREAT BRITAIN

R.N. OFFICERS' RANK INSIGNIA

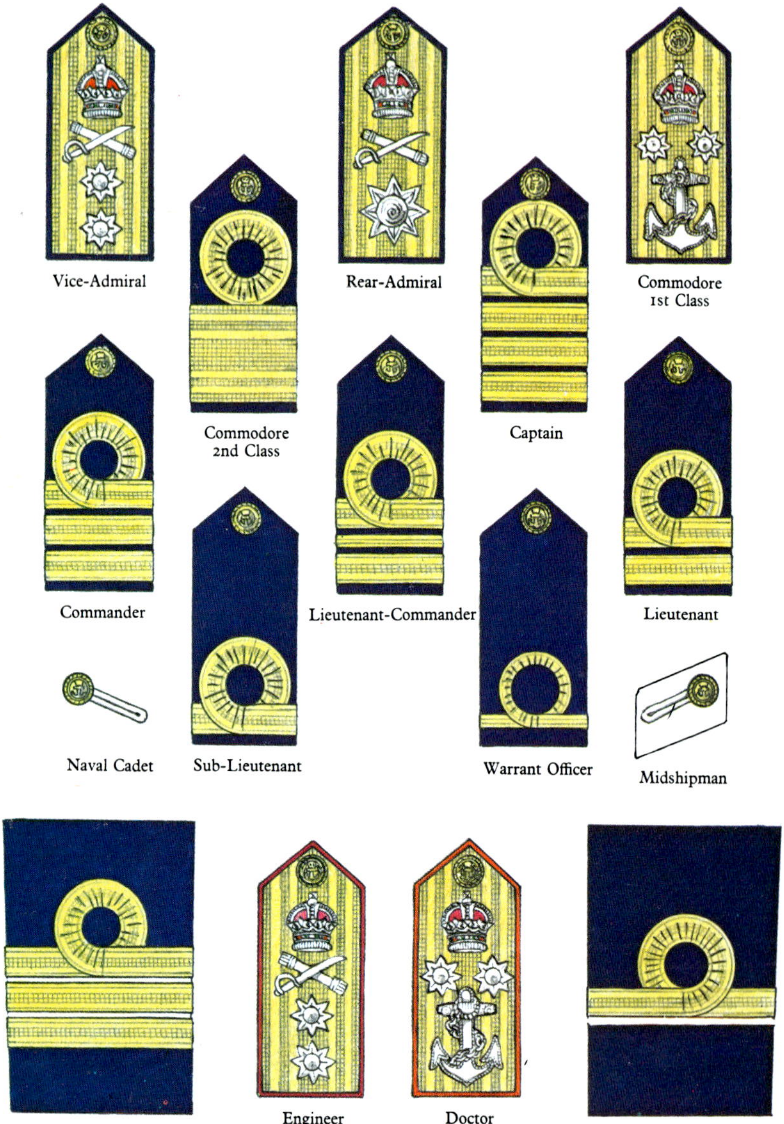

Vice-Admiral

Commodore 1st Class

Rear-Admiral

Commodore 1st Class

Commander

Commodore 2nd Class

Captain

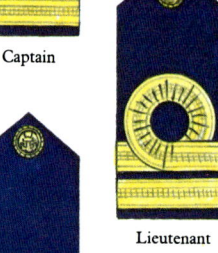
Lieutenant-Commander / Lieutenant

Naval Cadet

Sub-Lieutenant

Warrant Officer

Midshipman

Paymaster Commander

Engineer Vice-Admiral

Doctor Commodore 1st Class

Paymaster Sub-Lieutenant

PLATE 2

GREAT BRITAIN

R.N.R. OFFICERS' RANK INSIGNIA

Lieutenant-Commander

Commodore 2nd Class

Captain

Sub-Lieutenant

Commander

Lieutenant-Commander

Lieutenant

Sub-Lieutenant

Skipper

Paymaster Lieutenant-Commander

Paymaster Lieutenant-Commander

Paymaster Lieutenant

Midshipman   R.N.R. Cadet

Paymaster Lieutenant

PLATE 3

GREAT BRITAIN

R.N.V.R. OFFICERS' RANK INSIGNIA

Lieutenant-Commander

Commodore 2nd Class

Captain

Sub-Lieutenant

Commander

Lieutenant-Commander

Lieutenant

Sub-Lieutenant

Skipper

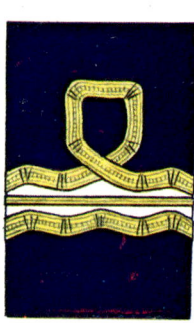
Paymaster Lieutenant-Commander

Paymaster Lieutenant-Commander

Paymaster Lieutenant

Midshipman

R.N.V.R. Cadet

Paymaster Lieutenant

PLATE 4

GREAT BRITAIN

R.N. BRANCH OFFICERS' RANK INSIGNIA

Air Branch Pilot

Instructor Commander

Commissioned Electrician

Air Branch Lieutenant

WOMEN'S ROYAL NAVAL SERVICE

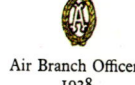
Observer

Officers' Cap Badge

Air Branch Officers 1938

Director

Chief Officer

1st Officer

Medical Superintendent

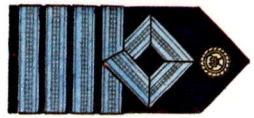
Deputy Director

2nd Officer

Chief Petty Officer

Petty Officer

Superintendent

3rd Officer

PLATE 5

GREAT BRITAIN

PETTY OFFICERS' AND NON-SUBSTANTIVE BADGES

Visual Signalman 1st Class

Stoker P.O.

Chief Petty Officer

Air Mechanic Ordnance

Leading Torpedoman (Low Power)

Regulating P.O.

Petty Officer

Leading Seaman

Wireman

Seaman Gunner Defensively Equipped Merchant Ships

Armourer's Mate

Chief Shipwright

Torpedo Coxwain Coastal Force Coxwain

Torpedo Gunner's Mate

Rangetaker 1st Class

Director Layer 1st Class Gunlayer 1st Class

Stoker Fire Fighter

PLATE 6

GREAT BRITAIN

NON-SUBSTANTIVE BADGES

Chief Rigger
Boom Defence

Chief Motor Mechanic

Surveying Recorder

Wireless Telegraphist
1st Class

Higher Submarine
Detector

Air Mechanic
(Engines)

Writer

Cook

Supply Rating

Air Fitter
(Electrical)

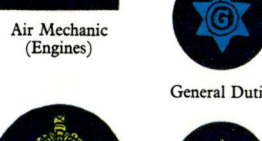
General Duties

Plotter
Bomb Range Marker

Officers' Steward

Gunner's Mate

Officers' Cook

Motor Driver
Despatch Rider

Chief Sailmaker

Bugler

Good Conduct Chevron
3 years

Coxwain

Telegraphist
Air Gunner 2nd Class

Diver

Combined Operations

Leading
Photographer

Phy. & Recreational
Training Instructor 2nd Class

GREAT BRITAIN

NON-SUBSTANTIVE BADGES

Sick Berth Rating   Signalman   Bomb Disposal   Sharpshooter   Master-at-Arms

CAP TALLIES

H.M.S. GLORIOUS.

H.M.S. COSSACK.

H.M.S. EFFINGHAM.

H.M.S. NEPTUNE.

H.M.S. VICTORY.

H.M.S. — Royal Navy

 — Royal Navy Youth Entries

S.A — South African Naval Forces

H.M.C.S. — Royal Canadian Navy

H.M.A.S. — Royal Australian Navy

H.M.N.Z.S. — Royal New Zealand Navy

H.M.I.S. — Royal Indian Navy

PLATE 8

GREAT BRITAIN

MERCHANT NAVY – ROYAL NATIONAL LIFEBOAT INSTITUTION

Chief Officer (Certified)

Merchant Navy

Officers' Cap Badge

Royal Naval Patrol Service

2nd Officer (Certified) Purser

Coxwain Royal National Lifeboat Institution

Captain (Certified Master)

Senior Surgeon

Other Ratings Royal National Lifeboat Institution

H.M. COASTGUARD

Chief Inspector

Inspectors', Higher Grades' and District Officers' Cap Badge

Station Officers

District Officers and Higher Grades

H.M.C.G. Other Ratings

Station Officers and Coastguardsmen

PLATE 9

GREAT BRITAIN
BADGES OF THE ROYAL MARINES

PLATE 10

GREAT BRITAIN

BADGES OF THE ROYAL MARINES

R.M. Division
116th R.M. Bde

34th Amphibian Support Regt

117th R.M. Bde

R.M. Engineers

104th R.M. Trng Bde
R.M. Trng Group

R.M. Shoulder Title

Bush Hat Flash
Far East 1944–45

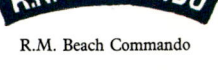

R.M. Beach Commando

44 R.M. Commando – embroidered

R.M. Siege Regiment

R.N. Personnel Attached
to R.M. Commandos

7th R.M. Bn
Shoulder Title
1943

40–48 R.M. Commando – woven

30th Assault Unit

CAP AND RANK INSIGNIA

U.S.S.R.

Flag Officers

Other Officers

Officers' Cap Badges
Line   Services

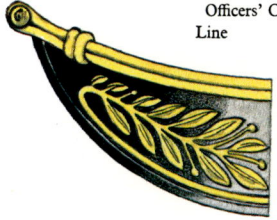 

Flag Officers   Captains

PLATE 11

U.S.S.R.

OFFICERS' RANK INSIGNIA

Marshal of the Fleet
of the Soviet Union (1955)

Admiral

Admiral of the Fleet

Admiral

Captain 2nd Rank

Captain-Lieutenant

Vice-Admiral

Rear-Admiral

Junior Lieutenant

Captain 1st Rank

Captain 2nd Rank

Captain 3rd Rank

Captain-Lieutenant

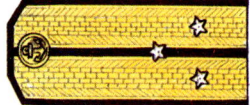
Senior Lieutenant

PLATE 12

U.S.S.R.

OFFICERS' RANK INSIGNIA

Lieutenant

Guards' Badge

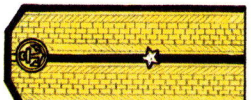
Junior Lieutenant

Flag Officers
Naval Aviation

Rear-Admiral
Line Engineering

Major-General
Aviation Engineering

Senior Officers
Supply

Colonel
Medical

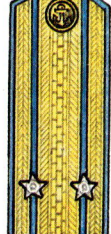
Lieutenant-Colonel
Naval Aviation

Major-General
Coast Defence

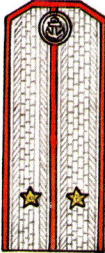
Lieutenant
Supply

Junior Lieutenant
Naval Constructions

Major-General
Administration

Major
Medical
(non-mil.trained)

Major
Veterinary

Captain
Legal

PLATE 13

U.S.S.R.

CAP AND RATE INSIGNIA

Midshipman

Chief Petty Officer

C.P.O.s' Cap Badge

Petty Officer 2nd Class
Black Sea Fleet

Leading Seaman
Caspian Sea Flotilla

Pacific Fleet

Arctic Fleet

Petty Officer 1st Class
Baltic Fleet

Amur River Flotilla

Volga River Flotilla

Lake Onega Flotilla

Advanced Engineering School

Junior Apprentice

Anti-Aircraft School

Coast Artillery School

Naval Political Institute

Lavanevski Naval Aviation School

Molotov Aviation Engineering School

Stalin Naval Aviation School

КРАСНЫЙ КАВКАЗ

Cap Tally

Marines

Belt Buckle

O.R.s' Cap Badge

PLATE 14

DENMARK

OFFICERS' CAP AND RANK INSIGNIA

Flag Officers

Senior Officers

Junior Officers

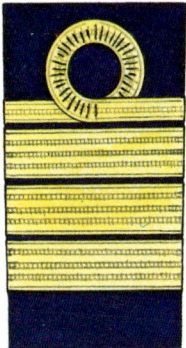
Admiral

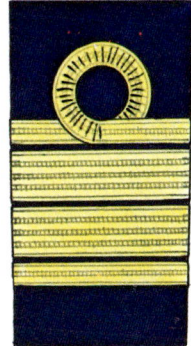
Vice-Admiral

Rear-Admiral

Kommandør

Kommandørkaptajn

Orlogskaptajn

Reserve

Aviation

Coast Artillery

DENMARK

OFFICERS' RANK INSIGNIA

Kaptajnløjtnant

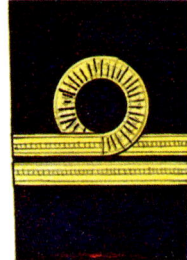
Soløjtnant af 1′ Gr.

Soløjtnant af 2′ Gr.

Naval Engineer
3rd Grade

Supply Intendant
2nd Grade

Reserve Doctor
Over 3 years Service

MIDSHIPMEN'S, CADETS' AND CHIEF PETTY OFFICERS' INSIGNIA

Midshipmen – Cadets
'A' Class

Reserve

Cap Badge

Coast Artillery

Midshipmen – Cadets
Ordinary

Medical

Engineers

Supply

C.P.O. 1st Grade

C.P.O. 2nd Grade

C.P.O. 3rd Grade

PLATE 16

DENMARK

PETTY OFFICERS' AND SEAMEN'S INSIGNIA

P.O. 1st Class

Petty Officers' Cap Badge

P.O. 2nd Class

TRADE BADGES

Apprentice Seaman

Cook – Storekeeper

Carpenter

Torpedo Mechanic

Signaller

Machinist – Stoker

Supplyman

Telegraphist

Sick Berth Orderly

Mechanic

Gunner

Mineman

Gunner Mechanic

Mine Mechanic

Torpedoman

Expert Rifleman

Expert Signaller

Seaman

Expert Gunner

Expert with Pistol

KGL. MARINE

Cap Tally

PLATE 17

GERMANY

CAP AND RANK INSIGNIA

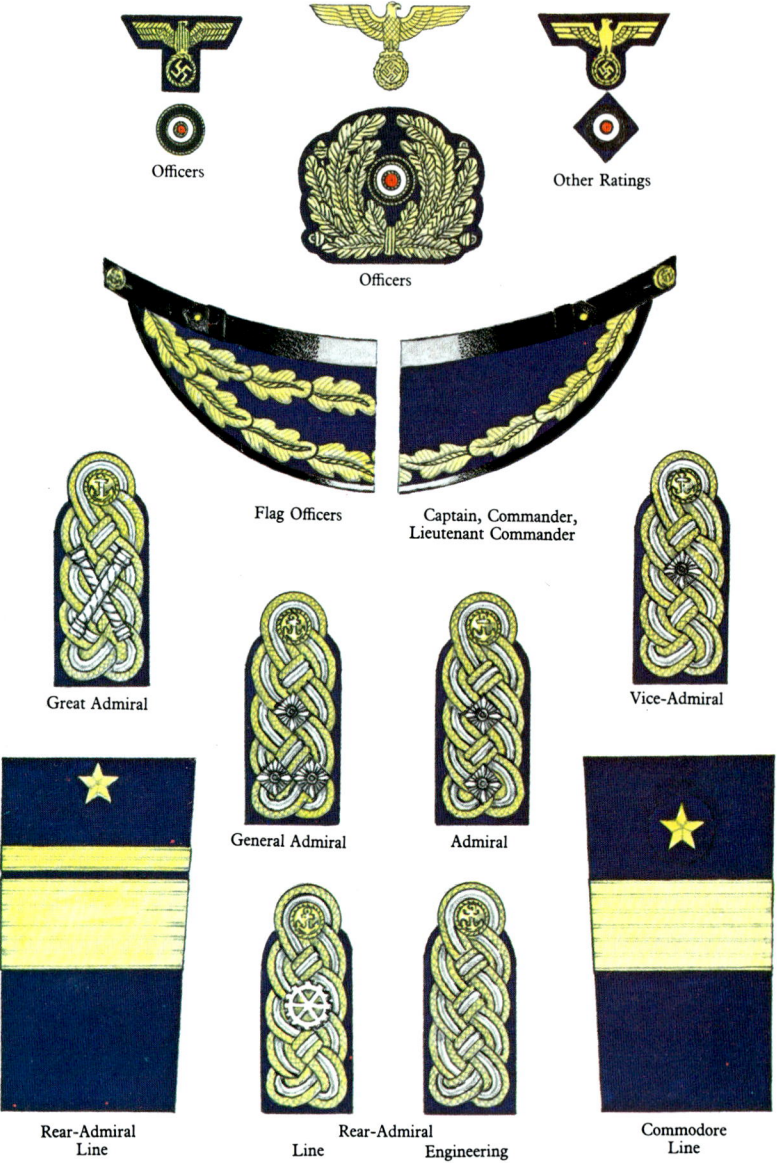

PLATE 18

GERMANY

OFFICERS' RANK INSIGNIA

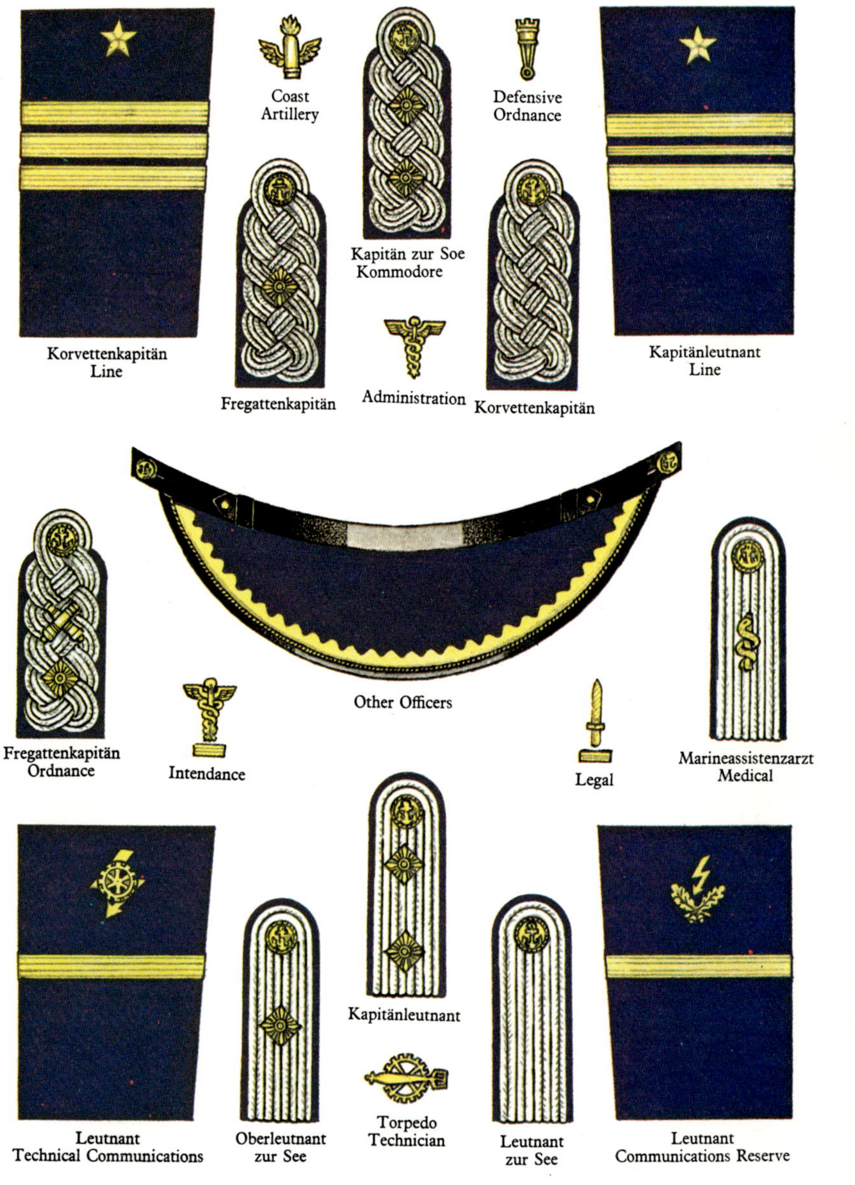

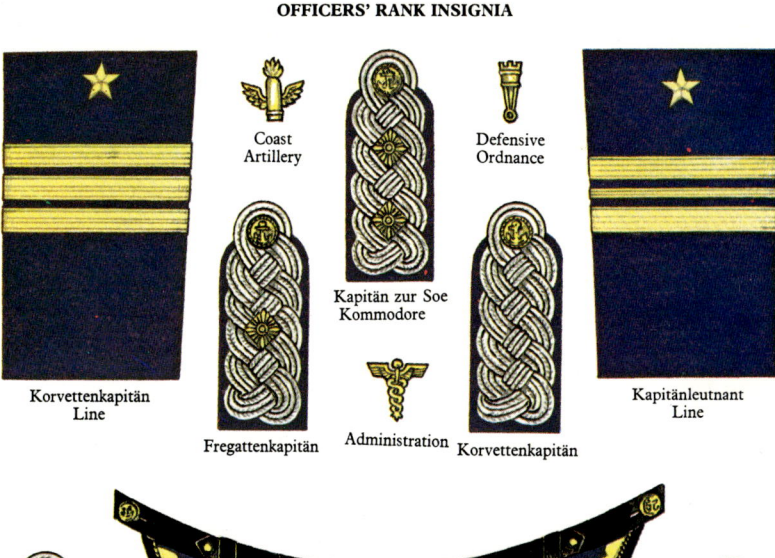

PLATE 19

GERMANY

BREAST INSIGNIA

Embroidered in gold

Woven in gold silk

Embroidered in yellow cotton

Metal

CHAPLAINS' BADGES

Cap and Collar Badges

MIDSHIPMEN'S AND CHIEF PETTY OFFICERS' RATE INSIGNIA

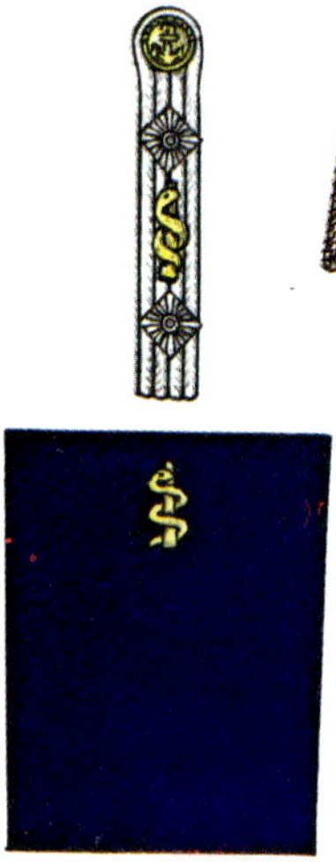

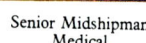
Senior Midshipman
Medical

Gunnery
Artificer

Defence
Ordnance

Gunnery

Midshipman
Line

Stabsoberbootsmann
Line

Stabsmaschinist
Engine Room

Stabssteuermann
Boatswain Branch

Schreiberfeldwebel
Clerical Dept

PLATE 20

GERMANY

PETTY OFFICERS' BADGES

Senior P.O. Line

P.O. Line

Signalman

Teleprinter

Radio Telegraphist

Writer

Carpenter

Aircraft Spotter

Driver

Gunner

Sick Berth Orderly

Torpedo Artificer

Boatswain

Gunnery Engineer

Defensive Ordnance Artificer

Gunnery Artificer

Engine Room Specialist

Hydrographer

Administrative Clerk

Bandsman

Candidate Officer Line

COLLAR PATCHES

Petty Officers

Seaman

Kriegsmarine

Cap Tally

GERMANY

DEPARTMENTAL BADGES

Line · Signals · Teleprinter · Radio Telegraph

Clerical · Carpentry · Aircraft Spotting · Motor Transport · Gunnery · Sick Berth

Torpedo Artificer · Gunnery Engineers · Defensive Ordnance · Gunnery Artificers · Engine Room Specialists · Administration

Band · Admirals' Staff · Hydrographer

SEAMEN'S RATE BADGES

Seaman 1st Class 8 years' Service

Seaman 1st Class 6 years' Service

Seaman 1st Class 4½ years' Service

Seaman 1st Class

Seaman 2nd Class Awaiting promotion to P.O.

Seaman 2nd Class Taking P.O. Training

Seaman 2nd Class

PLATE 22

GERMANY

WAR AWARDS AND CLASPS

- Destroyers
- Minesweepers, Anti-Sub. and Escort Vessels
- Submarines
- Coast Artillery
- Auxiliary Cruisers
- High-Sea Fleet
- Submarine Combat Clasp Bronze
- Blockade Runners
- Submarine Combat Clasp Silver
- Speed Boats
- Naval Combat Clasp
- Small Fighting Means 7th Class
- Small Fighting Means 6th Class
- Small Fighting Means 5th Class
- Small Fighting Means 4th Class
- Small Fighting Means 3rd Class
- Small Fighting Means 2nd Class
- Small Fighting Means 1st Class

CADETS' BADGES

- Line
- Engineers
- Ordnance
- Officials
- Medical
- Defensive Ordnance
- Administration

PLATE 23

GERMANY

TRADE BADGES

A.A. Gun Leader (Automatic)	 Gun Leader 'E' (Single Gun)	 Gun Leader 'T' (Turret) 3 years' Seniority	 Gun Leader 'E' 6 years' Seniority	 A.A. Gunner (Automatic)
 A.A. Gun Leader	 Artillery Specialist	 Anti-Aircraft Specialist	 Coast Artillery Specialist	 Coast Artillery Gun Leader
 Torpedo Master	 1st Class	 Torpedo Specialist 2nd Class	 3rd Class	 Torpedo Assistant Leader
 Range Taker	 A.A. Range Taker	 Mines Specialist	 A.A. Listener	 Searchlights Specialist Leader
 Ship Diver	 Torpedo Diver	Surveyor	 Motor Engineer 3rd Course	 Motor Engineer 2nd Course

PLATE 24

GERMANY

TRADE BADGES

Underwater Detector Specialist

Electrician 3rd Course

Electrician 2nd Course

Electrician 1st Course

Drummer – Piper

Underwater Detector Course

A.A. Detector Listener

P.T. Instructor

Gunnery Leader Coast Artillery

Drummer – Piper

BANDMASTERS

Music Master 1st type

Senior Music Superintendent

Music Superintendent

Music Master 2nd type

Staff Music Master

Senior Music Master

Music Master

PLATE 25

GERMANY

BADGES FOR FIELD GREY UNIFORM

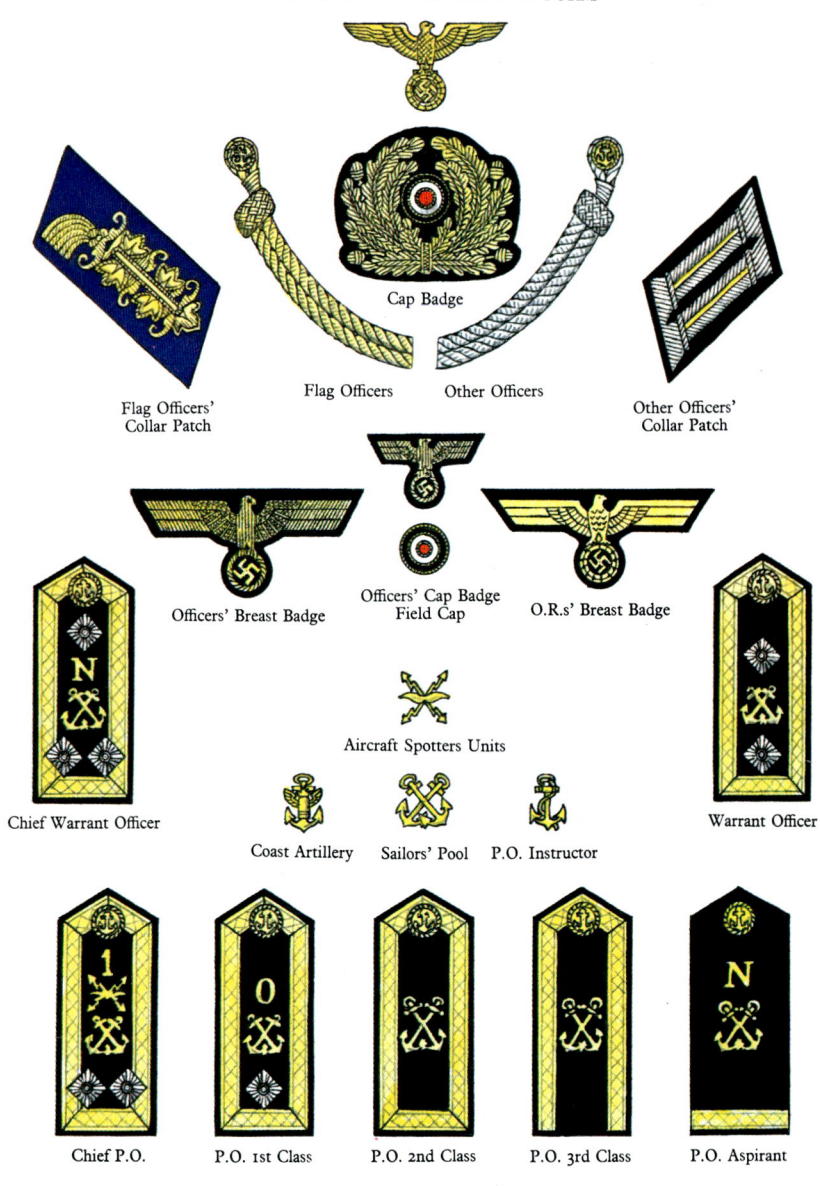

Cap Badge

Flag Officers' Collar Patch

Flag Officers

Other Officers

Other Officers' Collar Patch

Officers' Breast Badge

Officers' Cap Badge Field Cap

O.R.s' Breast Badge

Chief Warrant Officer

Aircraft Spotters Units

Coast Artillery

Sailors' Pool

P.O. Instructor

Warrant Officer

Chief P.O.

P.O. 1st Class

P.O. 2nd Class

P.O. 3rd Class

P.O. Aspirant

PLATE 26

GERMANY

OFFICIALS' INSIGNIA

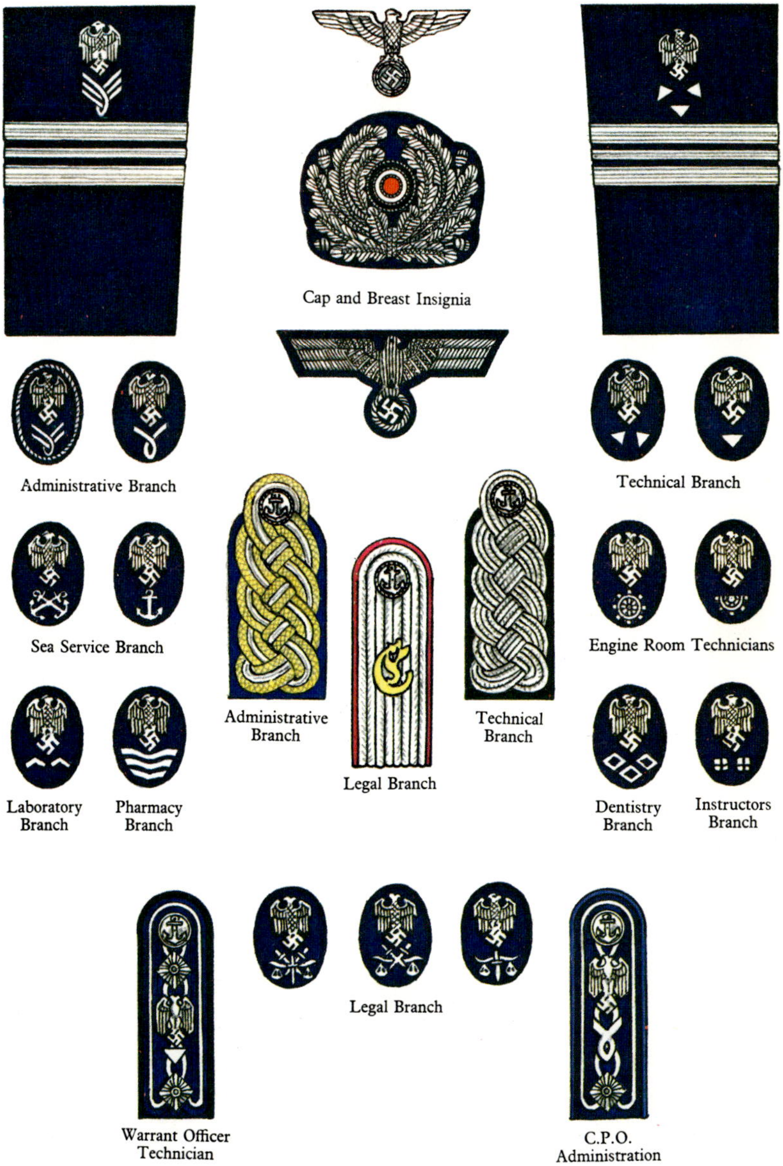

Cap and Breast Insignia

Administrative Branch

Technical Branch

Sea Service Branch

Engine Room Technicians

Administrative Branch

Legal Branch

Technical Branch

Laboratory Branch

Pharmacy Branch

Dentistry Branch

Instructors Branch

Warrant Officer Technician

Legal Branch

C.P.O. Administration

PLATE 27

FRANCE

FLAG OFFICERS' CAP AND RANK INSIGNIA

Flag Officers

Other Officers

Admiral of the Fleet, Admiral and Vice-Admiral of Squadron

Rear-Admiral

Shoulder Tabs

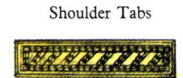

Flag Officers

Shoulder Tabs

Senior Officers

Junior Officers

Admiral of the Fleet

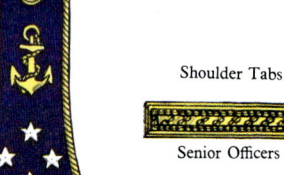

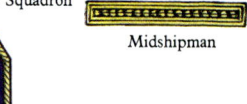

Admiral
Vice-Admiral of Squadron

Midshipman

Vice-Admiral

Rear-Admiral

Admiral
Vice-Admiral of Squadron

Flag Officers of Corps
Cap Badge

Rear-Admiral

PLATE 28

FRANCE

OFFICERS' CAP AND RANK INSIGNIA

Capitaine de Vaisseau

Capitaine de Vaisseau    Capitaine de Frégate

Capitaine de Corvette

Capitaine de Corvette   Lieutenant de Vaisseau

Enseigne de Vaisseau
de 1ère Classe

Enseigne de Vaisseau
de 2ème Classe

Officers' Cap Badge

Commissaire de 1ère Classe    Officier de 2ème Classe – Équipage de la Flotte

PLATE 29

FRANCE

CAP AND RATE INSIGNIA

Petty Officers' and Quartermasters' Cap Badges

Midshipman

Petty Officer

Chief Petty Officer

First Petty Officer

Second Petty Officer

Petty Officer

Quartermaster 2nd Class

Second Petty Officer 2 years' service-cadre

Auxiliary Guard

Quartermaster

Quartermaster 1st Class

Quartermaster 2nd Class

Qualified Seaman

PLATE 30

FRANCE

CAP, RATE AND SPECIALITY (ON COLLAR) INSIGNIA

Second Petty Officer Bugler

Fleet Pilot

Ratings' Cap Badge

Inspector and Auxiliary Guard

Bugler

Coast Signalman

Seaman Cap and Collar Badge

Fireman

Coast Signalman

Harbour Services

Pilot Chief of Section

Harbour Services

Fireman

Policeman

Policeman

Driver

Bandsman

SPECIALITY AND OTHER BADGES

P.T. Instructor

Aircraft Pilot

Airship Pilot

P.T. Instructor

Free French Navy

Ship's Badge

Aircraft Crew

Captive Balloon Observer

Free French Navy Seaman

PLATE 31

FRANCE

SPECIALITY INSIGNIA (ON SLEEVES)

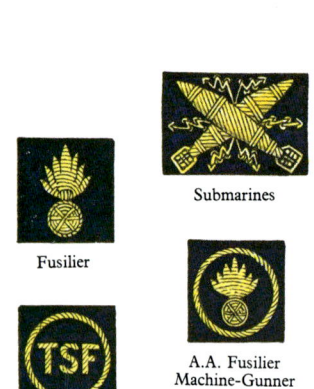

Ratings

Submarines

Submarines

Fusilier

Superior Certificate

Fusilier

A.A. Fusilier Machine-Gunner 1st Class

Fusilier Machine-Gunner Quartermaster Qualified Master Fusilier

Radio Telegraphist General Service

A.A. Fusilier Machine-Gunner

Radio Telegraphist Coastal

Facing Master

Facing Instructor

Recruited Bandsman

Auxiliary Fireman

Driver

Radio Signalman Shore Service

Gunlayer

Range Finder Operator

Aviation Personnel

Master Gunlayer

Gun Aimer

Aviation Radioman

Proficiency Stars for Layer and Aimer

F.N.F.L.

Free French Navy Cap Tally

PLATE 32

ITALY

HEAD-DRESS INSIGNIA

Port Captaincy

Great Admiral

Naval Ordnance

Admiral of Army (Fleet)

Rear-Admiral

Major Medical

Capitano di Corvetta Pharmacy

Major Naval Engineers

Captain Mechanical Engineers

Tenente di Vascello Line

Captain Naval Ordnance

Lieutenant Commissariat

1st, 2nd and 3rd Chief Line

Lieutenant Chaplains

PLATE 33

ITALY

FLAG OFFICERS' RANK INSIGNIA

Great Admiral

Great Admiral

Admiral of Army (Fleet)

Admiral of Army (Fleet)

Admiral of Squad in Command of Army

Rear-Admiral

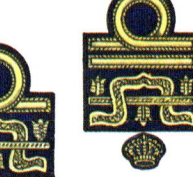

Admiral of Squad

Admiral of Division

Lieutenant-General Naval Engineers

Medical

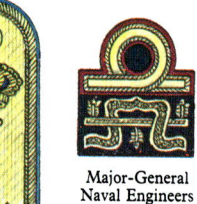

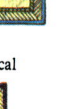

Major-General Naval Engineers

Lieutenant-General Port Captaincy

Commissariat

Line

Submarine Officer

Medical

Admiral of Squad

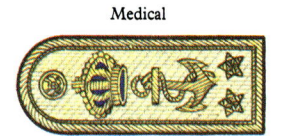

Admiral of Division

Naval Engineers

Rear-Admiral

Commissariat

PLATE 34

ITALY

OFFICERS' RANK INSIGNIA

Capitano di Vascello

Capitano di Vascello

Capitano di Fregata

Capitano di Fregata    Capitano di Corvetta    Tenente di Vascello    Sottotenente di Vascello    Guardiamarina

Senior Officers Line

Senior Officers Medical

Major Medical

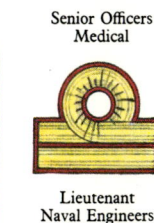

Lieutenant Naval Engineers

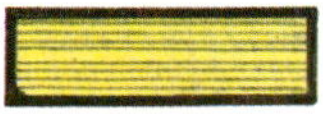

Junior Officers Line

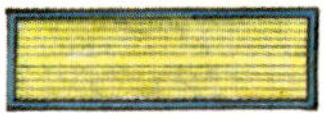

Capitano di Corvetta    1° Tenente di Vascello    Tenente di Vascello

Junior Officers Medical

Mechanical Services

Technical Services

Accountancy Services   1° Sottotenente di Vascello    Sottotenente di Vascello    Guardiamarina

Directors of Music

PLATE 35

ITALY

PETTY OFFICERS' RATE INSIGNIA AND TRADE BADGES

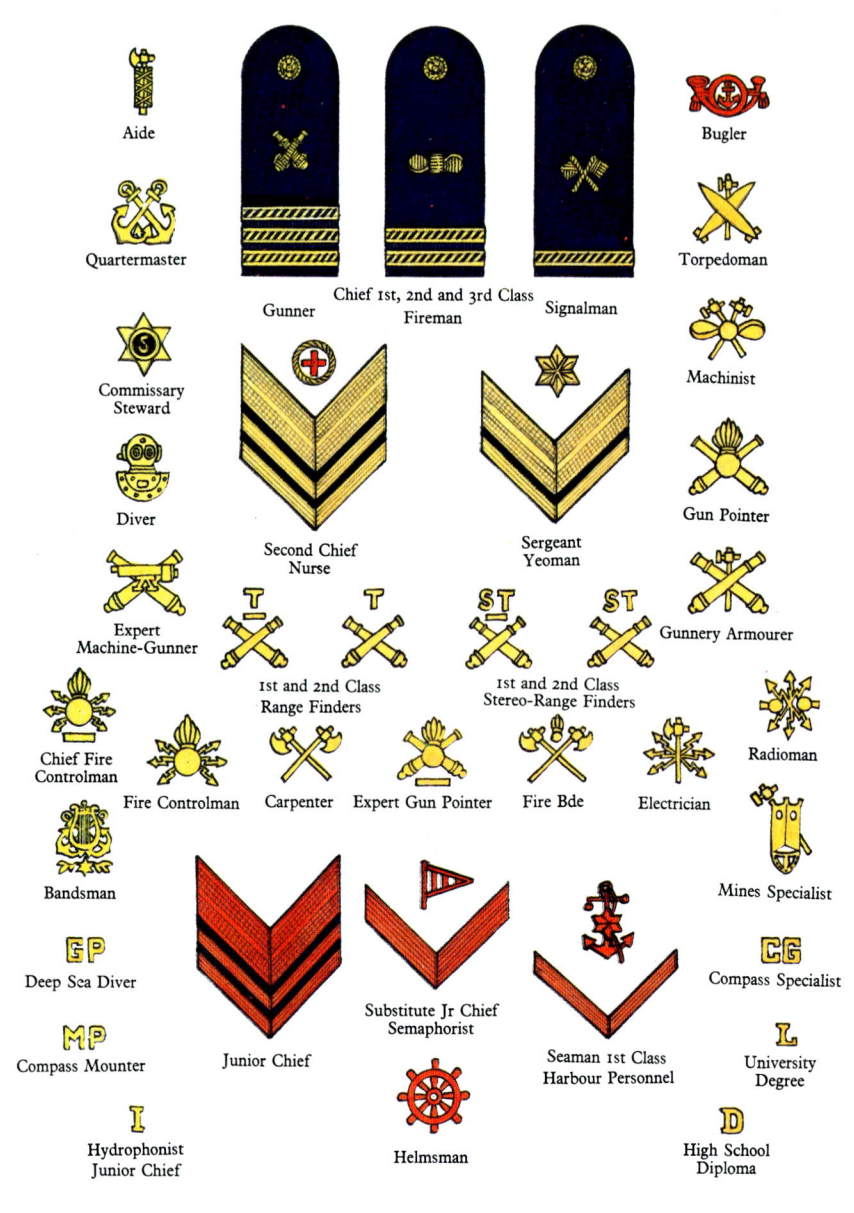

Aide

Quartermaster

Commissary Steward

Diver

Expert Machine-Gunner

Chief Fire Controlman

Fire Controlman

Bandsman

Deep Sea Diver

Compass Mounter

Hydrophonist Junior Chief

Gunner

Chief 1st, 2nd and 3rd Class Fireman

Signalman

Second Chief Nurse

Sergeant Yeoman

1st and 2nd Class Range Finders

1st and 2nd Class Stereo-Range Finders

Carpenter

Expert Gun Pointer

Fire Bde

Electrician

Junior Chief

Substitute Jr Chief Semaphorist

Helmsman

Seaman 1st Class Harbour Personnel

Bugler

Torpedoman

Machinist

Gun Pointer

Gunnery Armourer

Radioman

Mines Specialist

Compass Specialist

University Degree

High School Diploma

PLATE 36

ITALY

TRADE BADGES

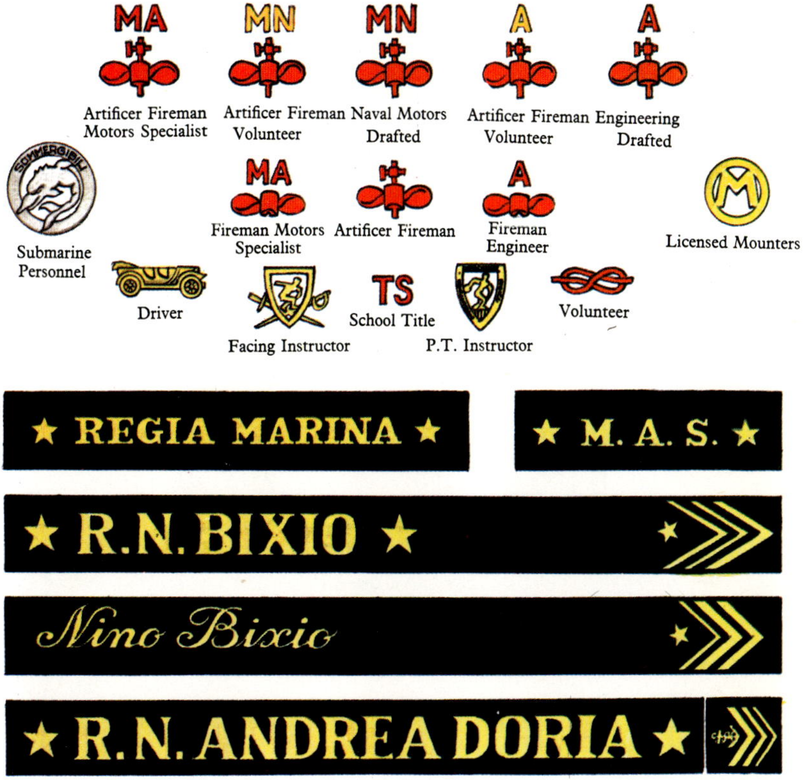

- **MA** — Artificer Fireman Motors Specialist
- **MN** — Artificer Fireman Volunteer
- **MN** — Naval Motors Drafted
- **A** — Artificer Fireman Engineering Volunteer
- **A** — Engineering Drafted
- Submarine Personnel
- **MA** — Fireman Motors Specialist
- Artificer Fireman
- **A** — Fireman Engineer
- Licensed Mounters
- Driver
- Facing Instructor
- **TS** — School Title
- P.T. Instructor
- Volunteer

★ REGIA MARINA ★   ★ M. A. S. ★

★ R.N. BIXIO ★

Nino Bixio

★ R.N. ANDREA DORIA ★

BADGES OF 'SAN MARCO' MARINES

- Officers' Collar Patch
- O.R.s' Cap Badge
- Sleeve Badge
- Folgore Combat Group
- O.R.s' Cuff Patch
- Parachute Brevet Badge (N.P. Bn)
- San Marco Regt – Bafile Bn
- Officers' Collar Patch

PLATE 37

ITALY

NAVAL BADGES AND INSIGNIA OF THE ITALIAN SOCIAL REPUBLIC

Officers' Cap Badges

O.R.s' Cap Badge

Flag Officers

Admiral

Capitano di Corvetta

Sottotenente di Vascello

Anti-Submarine Group – La Spezia

Dredging Flotilla Venice

WAR NAVIGATION BADGES (2ND DEGREE)

Submarine Atlantic Base

Battle Ships

Cruisers

Torpedo Ships

Pilot Surface Assault Craft

Pilot Underwater Assault Craft

Submarines

Anti-Submarine Vessels

M.A.S.

Fulmine Bn

Assault Crafts

Auxiliary Ships

Hospital Ships

PLATE 38

ITALY

NAVAL BADGES AND INSIGNIA OF THE ITALIAN SOCIAL REPUBLIC

Generals' Collar Badge

Xth M.A.S. Infantry

All Other Ranks' Collar Badge

San Marco – Military Police

Xth M.A.S. Infantry

San Marco

Lupo Bn

Training in Germany

San Marco – Artillery

Swimming Brevet

Barbarigo Bn

Adriatic Front

San Marco Reconnaissance

Para-Swimmers

Valanga Bn

Sagittario Bn

Xth Flotilla M.A.S.

Xth M.A.S. Naval Assault

Artillery

Xth M.A.S. Infantry

Xth Division M.A.S.

PLATE 39

U.S.A.

HEAD-DRESS INSIGNIA

Officers' Cap Badge
(post-1941)

Officers' Cap Badge
(pre-1941)

Officers' Cap Badge
(embroidered)

Flag Officers   Captain and Commander

Officers'
Garrison Cap

Warrant Officers

Nurse

U.S. Navy Aviators'
Garrison Cap

Petty Officers

Midshipman

Warrant Officers'
Pharmacist – Garrison Cap

Officers' Cook and Steward

Officers' Cap Badge
U.S.C.G.

Officers' Steward

Warrant Officers
U.S.C.G.

Petty Officers
U.S.C.G.

Surfman

Cadet
U.S.C.G.

Shore Establishment
U.S.C.G.

PLATE 40

U.S.A.

OFFICERS' RANK AND CORPS INSIGNIA

Admiral of the Fleet Admiral Vice Admiral Rear Admiral Commodore

Captain
Line

Chaplain
Jewish

Band

Admiral
Line

Lieutenant
Civil Engineering
Corps

Commander
Chaplain – Christian

Hospital

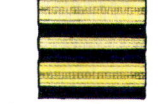

Lieutenant Commander
Supply Corps

Lieutenant Commander
Dental Corps

Lieutenant (Junior Gr.)
Medical Corps

Ensign
Navy Nurse Corps

Ensign
U.S. Coast Guard

PLATE 41

U.S.A.

WARRANT OFFICERS' RANK AND CORPS INSIGNIA

Boatswain

Gunner

Carpenter

Ship's Clerk

Torpedoman

Chief Warrant Officer
Aerographer

Warrant Officer
U.S.C.G. Pay Clerk

Radio Electrician

Machinist

Electrician

Photographer

Pharmacist

OFFICERS' MINIATURE RANK AND CORPS INSIGNIA

Admiral
of the Fleet

Admiral

Vice Admiral

Rear Admiral

Commodore

Captain

Commander

Lieutenant Commander

Lieutenant

Lieutenant
(Junior Grade)

Ensign

Supply

Dental

Chaplain
Christian

Chaplain
Jewish

Medical

Civil Engineering

PLATE 42

U.S.A.

INSIGNIA FOR PETTY OFFICERS

Chief Petty Officer
Electrician's Mate
12 years with Good Conduct

Chief Petty Officer
Radioman
8 years

Chief Petty Officer
Turret Captain
4 years

Petty Officer 1st Class
Carpenter's Mate

Petty Officer 2nd Class
Signalman

Petty Officer 3rd Class
Quartermaster

CUFF MARKINGS

Seaman/Fireman 1st Class

Construction
Battalions

Minecraft
Personnel

Seaman/Fireman 2nd Class   Apprentice Seaman/Fireman 3rd Class

PLATE 43

U.S.A.

CAP TALLIES

U.S. NAVY — U.S. Navy

U.S. COAST GUARD — U.S. Coast Guard

SPECIALITY MARKS

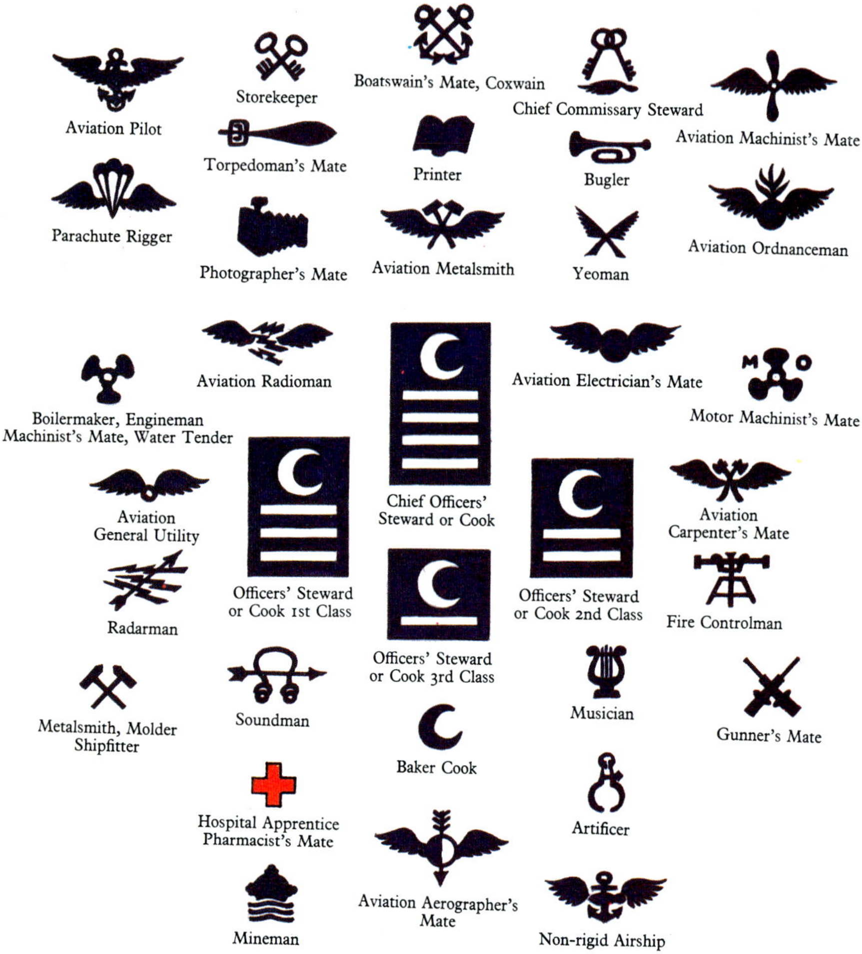

- Aviation Pilot
- Storekeeper
- Boatswain's Mate, Coxwain
- Chief Commissary Steward
- Aviation Machinist's Mate
- Torpedoman's Mate
- Printer
- Bugler
- Parachute Rigger
- Photographer's Mate
- Aviation Metalsmith
- Yeoman
- Aviation Ordnanceman
- Aviation Radioman
- Aviation Electrician's Mate
- Boilermaker, Engineman, Machinist's Mate, Water Tender
- Motor Machinist's Mate
- Aviation General Utility
- Chief Officers' Steward or Cook
- Aviation Carpenter's Mate
- Radarman
- Officers' Steward or Cook 1st Class
- Officers' Steward or Cook 2nd Class
- Fire Controlman
- Metalsmith, Molder, Shipfitter
- Soundman
- Officers' Steward or Cook 3rd Class
- Musician
- Gunner's Mate
- Baker Cook
- Hospital Apprentice Pharmacist's Mate
- Artificer
- Mineman
- Aviation Aerographer's Mate
- Non-rigid Airship

PLATE 44

U.S.A.

DISTINGUISHING MARKS AND SPECIALIST RATINGS

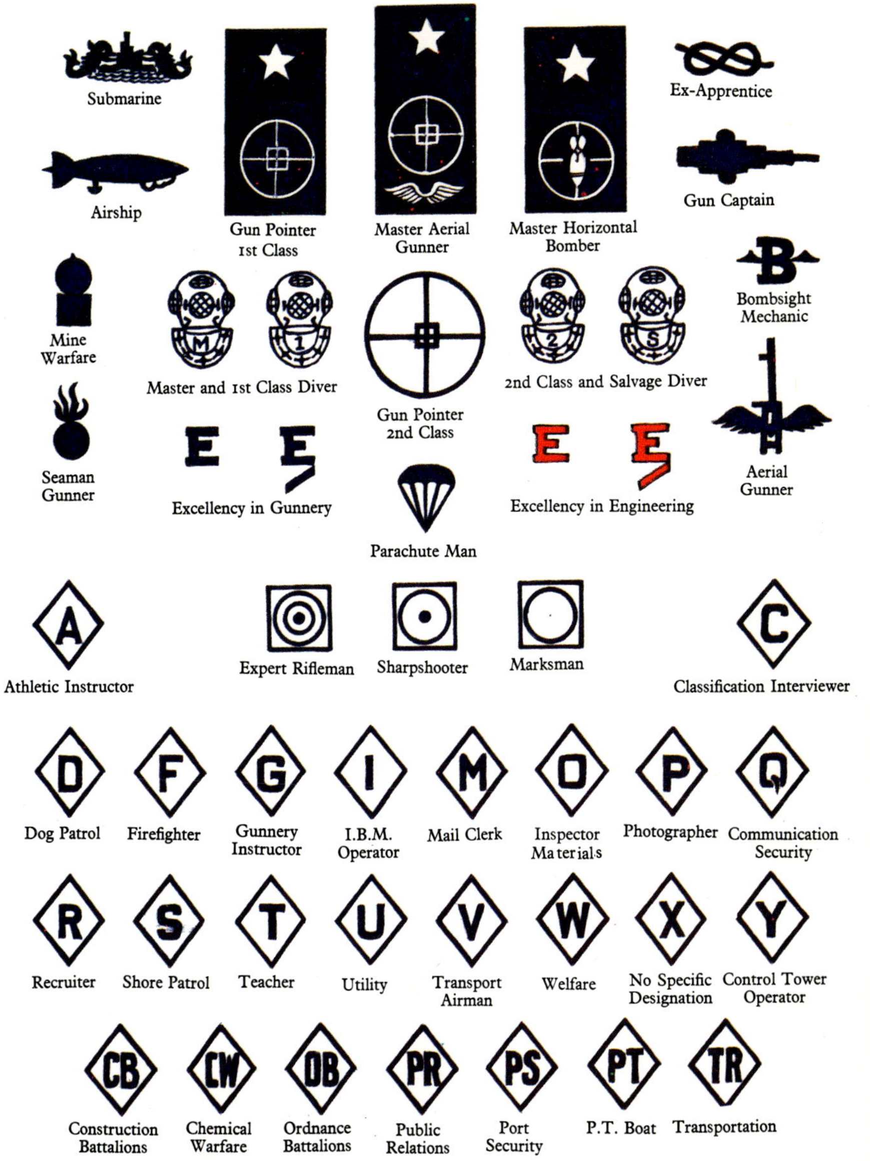

	Submarine
	Airship
	Gun Pointer 1st Class
	Master Aerial Gunner
	Master Horizontal Bomber
	Ex-Apprentice
	Gun Captain
	Mine Warfare
	Master and 1st Class Diver
	Gun Pointer 2nd Class
	2nd Class and Salvage Diver
	Bombsight Mechanic
	Seaman Gunner
	Excellency in Gunnery
	Excellency in Engineering
	Aerial Gunner
	Parachute Man
A	Athletic Instructor
	Expert Rifleman
	Sharpshooter
	Marksman
C	Classification Interviewer
D	Dog Patrol
F	Firefighter
G	Gunnery Instructor
I	I.B.M. Operator
M	Mail Clerk
O	Inspector Materials
P	Photographer
Q	Communication Security
R	Recruiter
S	Shore Patrol
T	Teacher
U	Utility
V	Transport Airman
W	Welfare
X	No Specific Designation
Y	Control Tower Operator
CB	Construction Battalions
CW	Chemical Warfare
OB	Ordnance Battalions
PR	Public Relations
PS	Port Security
PT	P.T. Boat
TR	Transportation

PLATE 45

U.S.A.

QUALIFICATION BADGES

Naval Aviator

Balloon Pilot

Aviation Observer

Submarine Officer

Submarine Surgeon

Submarine Combat Insignia

Flight Surgeon

Air Crew Member

Tactical Observer

Navigator

Radar Observer

MISCELLANEA

Shore Patrol

Geneva Cross

Amphibious Forces

Honorable Discharge

Seaman Guard

U.S.N. Officers

U.S.N. Enlisted Men

WAVES

U.S.N. Enlisted Men

U.S.M.C.

U.S.C.G.

PLATE 46

U.S.A.

U.S.M.C. HEAD-DRESS AND COLLAR, CORPS AND RANK INSIGNIA

Officers – Dress | Officers – Service | Enlisted Men – Dress | Enlisted Men – Service

Officers – Garrison Cap | Aviation Cadet | Enlisted Men – Garrison Cap

Aide to Brigadier General Dress | Adjutant and Inspector's Department – Dress | Aviation Cadet Dress | Paymaster's Department Dress | Aide to Major General Service

Quartermaster's Department Dress

General | Lieutenant General | Major General | Brigadier General | Colonel

Adjutant and Inspector's Department – Service | Lieutenant Colonel | Major | Paymaster's Department Service

Captain | 1st Lieutenant | 2nd Lieutenant

PLATE 47

U.S.A.

U.S.M.C. WARRANT OFFICERS' RANK AND CORPS INSIGNIA

Marine Gunner Dress

Chief Warrant Officer

Chief Warrant Officer Paymaster's Dept

Second Leader Marine Band

Marine Gunner Service

DISTINGUISHING MARKS

Gun Pointer 1st Class

Gun Pointer 2nd Class

Navy 'E'

Gun Captain

SHOULDER SLEEVE INSIGNIA   1ST MARINE AMPHIBIOUS CORPS

Corps, Anti-Tank Bns, 155 Howitzer Bn

Artillery

Balloon Barrage Bns

Paratroopers

Defense Bns

Raiders

Service Supply

Aviation Engineers

PLATE 48

U.S.A.

U.S.M.C. N.C.O.s' RANK INSIGNIA

First Sergeant

1st Grade Line

Band Leader

1st Grade Staff

2nd Grade Line

2nd Grade Staff

3rd Grade Line

3rd Grade Staff

4th Grade

5th Grade

6th Grade

Musician P.F.C.

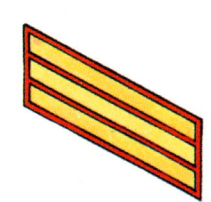

Service Stripes
12 years

Musician

PLATE 49

U.S.A.

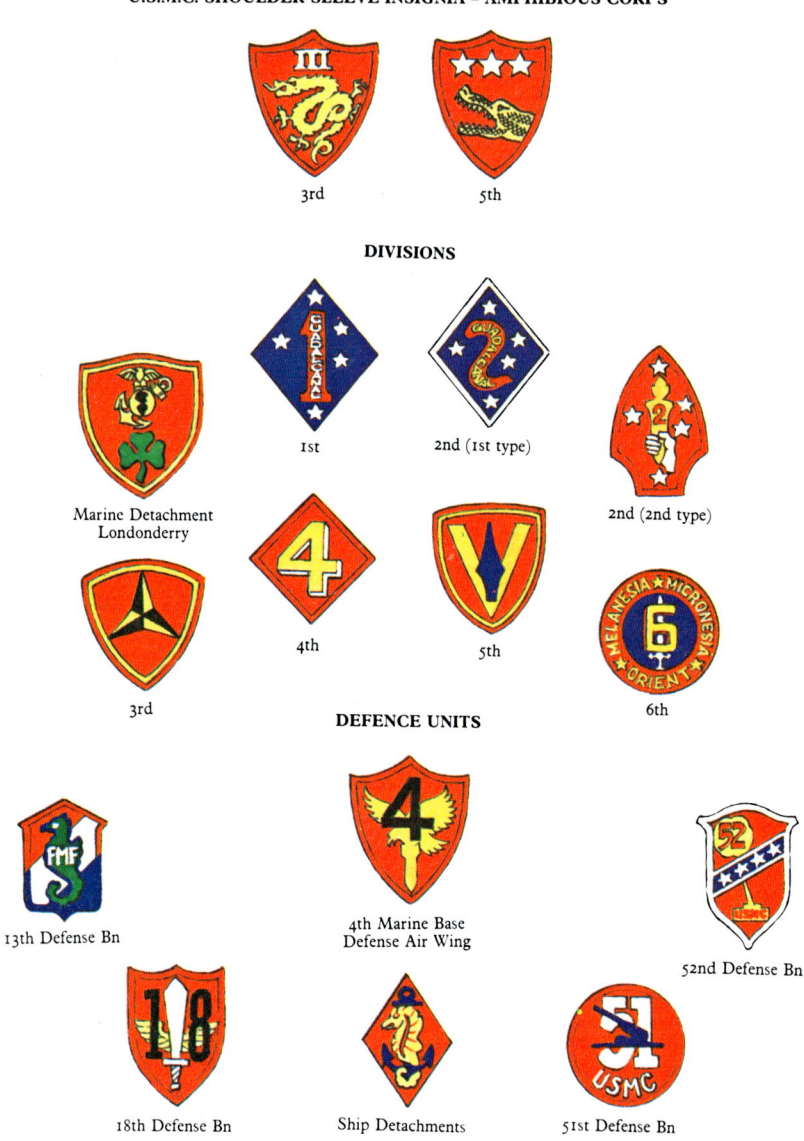

U.S.M.C. SHOULDER SLEEVE INSIGNIA – AMPHIBIOUS CORPS

3rd   5th

DIVISIONS

1st   2nd (1st type)

Marine Detachment
Londonderry

2nd (2nd type)

4th   5th

3rd   6th

DEFENCE UNITS

13th Defense Bn

4th Marine Base
Defense Air Wing

52nd Defense Bn

18th Defense Bn   Ship Detachments   51st Defense Bn

PLATE 50

U.S.A.

U.S.M.C. SHOULDER SLEEVE INSIGNIA – FLEET MARINE FORCES

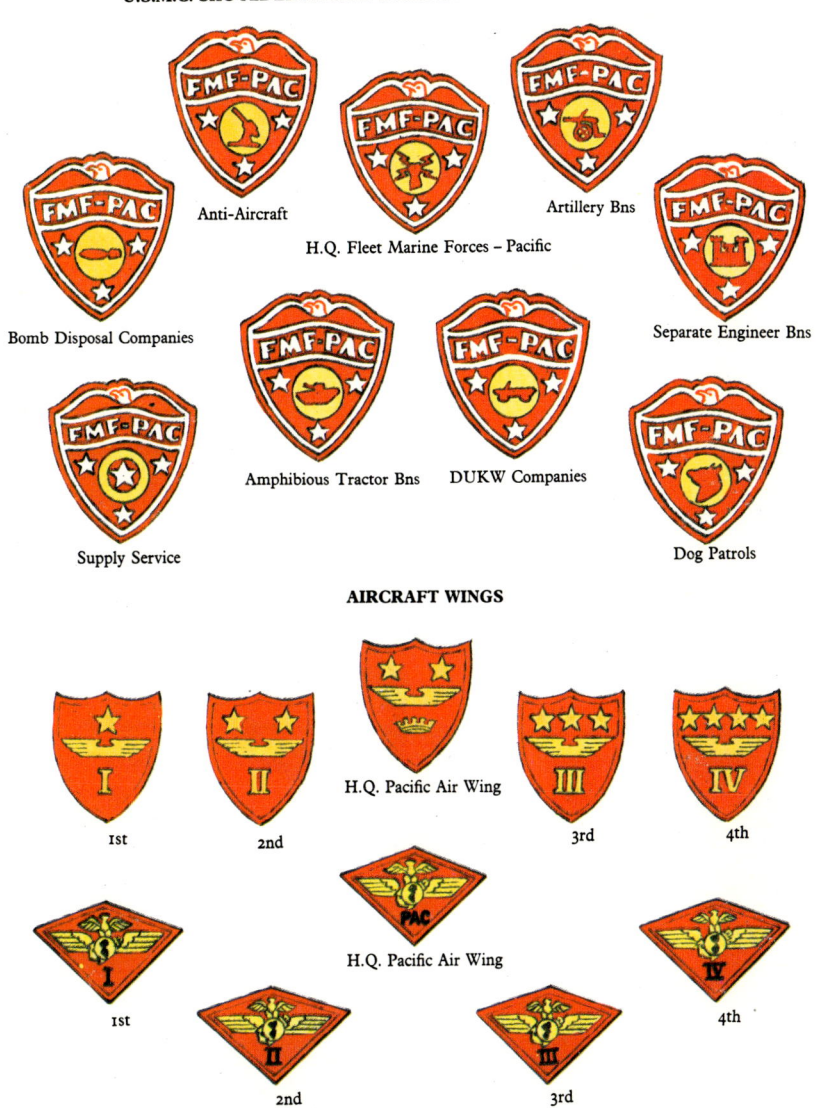

Anti-Aircraft

H.Q. Fleet Marine Forces – Pacific

Artillery Bns

Bomb Disposal Companies

Separate Engineer Bns

Amphibious Tractor Bns

DUKW Companies

Supply Service

Dog Patrols

AIRCRAFT WINGS

1st

2nd

H.Q. Pacific Air Wing

3rd

4th

1st

H.Q. Pacific Air Wing

4th

2nd

3rd

PLATE 51

U.S.A.

SUBSIDIARY SERVICES

- Master A.T.S.
- Officers' Cap Badge A.T.S.
- Collar Badge A.T.S.
- Officers' Cap Badge M.S.
- Lieutenant M.S.
- P.O.s' Cap Badge Master at Arms A.T.S.
- Collar Badge A.T.S.
- C.P.O.s' Cap Badge M.S.
- Lapel Badge Radioman A.T.S.
- Lapel Badge Transportation Agent A.T.S.
- Signalman M.S.
- Wheelman A.T.S.
- Officers' Garrison Cap Badge C. & G.S.
- P.O. 3rd Class Storekeeper – M.S.
- Officers' Cap Badge C. & G.S.
- Electrician C. & G.S.
- Mate C. & G.S.
- P.O. 1st Class Oiler C. & G.S.
- Cap Badge P.H.S.
- Commander C. & G.S.
- Officers' Steward or Cook Cap Badge – C. & G.S.
- U.S. Cadet Nurse Corps
- Acting Assistant Surgeon – P.H.S.
- Cap Tally
- Passed Assistant Surgeon – P.H.S.

PLATE 52

JAPAN

CAP BADGES

Midshipmen and Cadets
Line

Officers
Peaked Cap

Petty Officers
(embroidered)

Steel Helmet

All Ranks
Field Cap and Helmet
1st type

Steel Helmet

Seamen
White Cap

Petty Officers
(metal)

All except Seamen
Field Cap

大日本帝國海軍

Cap Tally

OFFICERS' RANK INSIGNIA

Admiral

Vice Admiral

Rear Admiral

PLATE 53

JAPAN

OFFICERS' RANK INSIGNIA

Captain   Commander   Lieutenant-Commander

Lieutenant   Sub-Lieutenant   Ensign

Midshipman
Warrant Officer   Midshipman   Cadet   Warrant Officer   Cadet

PLATE 54

JAPAN

RANK INSIGNIA – COLLAR PATCHES

Admiral	 Vice Admiral	 Rear Admiral	 Captain
 Commander	 Lieutenant-Commander	 Lieutenant	 Sub-Lieutenant
 Ensign	 Midshipman	 Cadet	 Warrant Officer

RANK INSIGNIA – OFFICERS COMMISSIONED FROM THE RANKS

Lieutenant

Sub-Lieutenant

Ensign

Warrant Officer

PLATE 55

JAPAN

PETTY OFFICERS' RATE BADGES (1ST TYPE)

Line 1st Class	 Engineer 1st Class	 Aviation 1st Class	 Ordnance 1st Class	 Administration 1st Class
 Line 2nd Class	 Engineer 2nd Class	 Aviation 2nd Class	 Ordnance 2nd Class	 Administration 2nd Class
 Line 3rd Class	 Engineer 3rd Class	 Aviation 3rd Class	 Ordnance 3rd Class	 Administration 3rd Class

SEAMEN'S RATE INSIGNIA

Line 1st Class	 Engineer 1st Class	 Aviation 1st Class	 Ordnance 1st Class	 Administration 1st Class
 Line 2nd Class	 Engineer 2nd Class	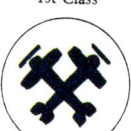 Aviation 2nd Class	 Ordnance 2nd Class	 Administration 2nd Class
 Line 3rd Class	 Engineer 3rd Class	 Aviation 3rd Class	 Ordnance 3rd Class	 Administration 3rd Class

PLATE 56

JAPAN

PETTY OFFICERS' AND SEAMENS' RATE BADGES (1ST TYPE)

Musician 1st Class

Musician 2nd Class

Musician 3rd Class

Examples of various aviation badges

Musician 1st Class

Musician 2nd Class

Musician 3rd Class

GOOD CONDUCT CHEVRONS (1ST TYPE)

Good Conduct according to duration of service

Excellent Conduct

OTHER BADGES

Fighter Aircraft

Medical

Bomber Aircraft

Naval Collar Patch

Parachute Troops

Naval Aviation Collar Patch

PLATE 57

JAPAN

RANK INSIGNIA – OFFICERS OF THE CORPS

Commander Paymaster

Captain Construction

Ensign Survey

Commander Medical

Commander Paymaster

Warrant Officer Carpenter

Sub-Lieutenant Engineer

Commander Line

GOOD CONDUCT CHEVRONS, PETTY OFFICERS' AND SEAMENS' RATE INSIGNIA (2ND TYPE)

Commander Justice

Good Conduct

Excellent Conduct

Special Training

P.O. 1st Class Line

P.O. 2nd Class Engineer

P.O. 3rd Class Justice Clerk

Advanced Special Training

Seaman 1st Class Sick Berth

Seaman 2nd Class Hydrographer

Seaman 3rd Class Paymaster Clerk

PLATE 58

POLAND

CAP AND RANK INSIGNIA

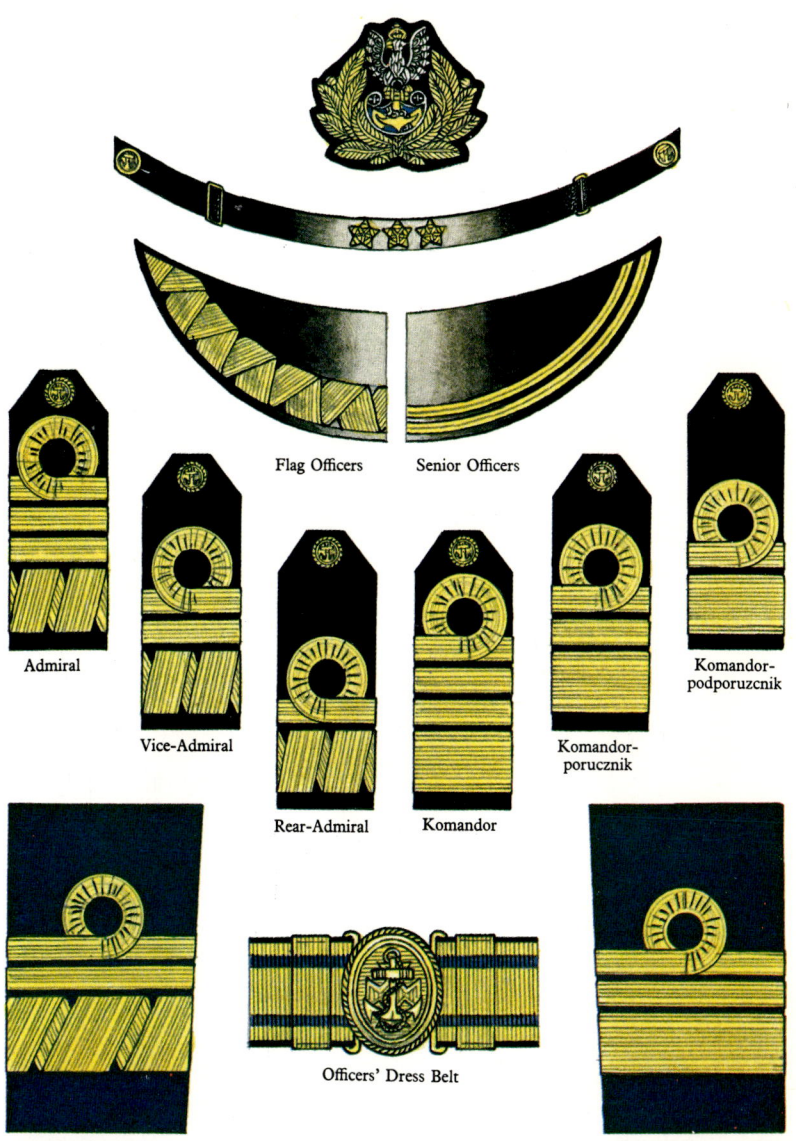

Flag Officers Senior Officers

Admiral

Vice-Admiral

Rear-Admiral

Komandor

Komandor-porucznik

Komandor-podporucznik

Vice-Admiral

Officers' Dress Belt

Komandor-porucznik

PLATE 59

POLAND

CAP AND RANK INSIGNIA

Porucznik

Junior Officers

Kapitan

Kapitan  Porucznik

Podporucznik Medical

Warrant Officer

Podporucznik Administration

Chief Petty Officer 1st Class

Warrant Officer

P.O.s' Cap Badge

Chief Petty Officer 1st Class

PLATE 60

POLAND

CAP, RATE AND TRADE INSIGNIA

C.P.O. Reserve Cadet	Chief Petty Officer	C.P.O. Cadet
Helmsman	Chief Petty Officer	Mechanician
Signalman		Gunner
Electrician	Other Ratings' Cap Badges	Seaman

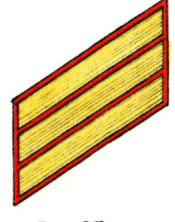

Petty Officer	Leading Seaman	Able Seaman

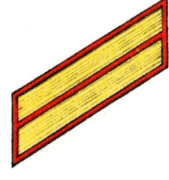

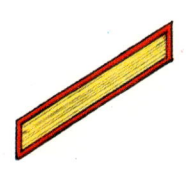

PLATE 61

POLAND

CAP TALLIES

MARYNARKA WOJENNA

O.R.P. GDYNIA.

TRADE BADGES

Range Finder Operator	 Torpedo – Mineman	 Writer	 Plotter
 Ordnance Artificer	 Shipwright	 Seaman Gunner	 Carpenter
 Photographer	 Radio Telegraphist	 Wireless Operator	 Cook
 Administrative Clerk	 Stoker	 Writer	 Rifleman
 Coxwain	 Sick Berth Rating	 Bandsman	 Diver

PLATE 62

NETHERLANDS

CAP AND RANK INSIGNIA

Line

Engineering

Aviation

Officers' Cap Insignia

Flag Officers

Captain, Commander

Admiral

Medical

Administration

Vice-Admiral

Chaplains

Admiral

W.O.s and P.O.s

Yeoman

Musicians

Kapitein-Luitenant ter Zee

PLATE 63

NETHERLANDS

RANK INSIGNIA AND COLLAR BADGES

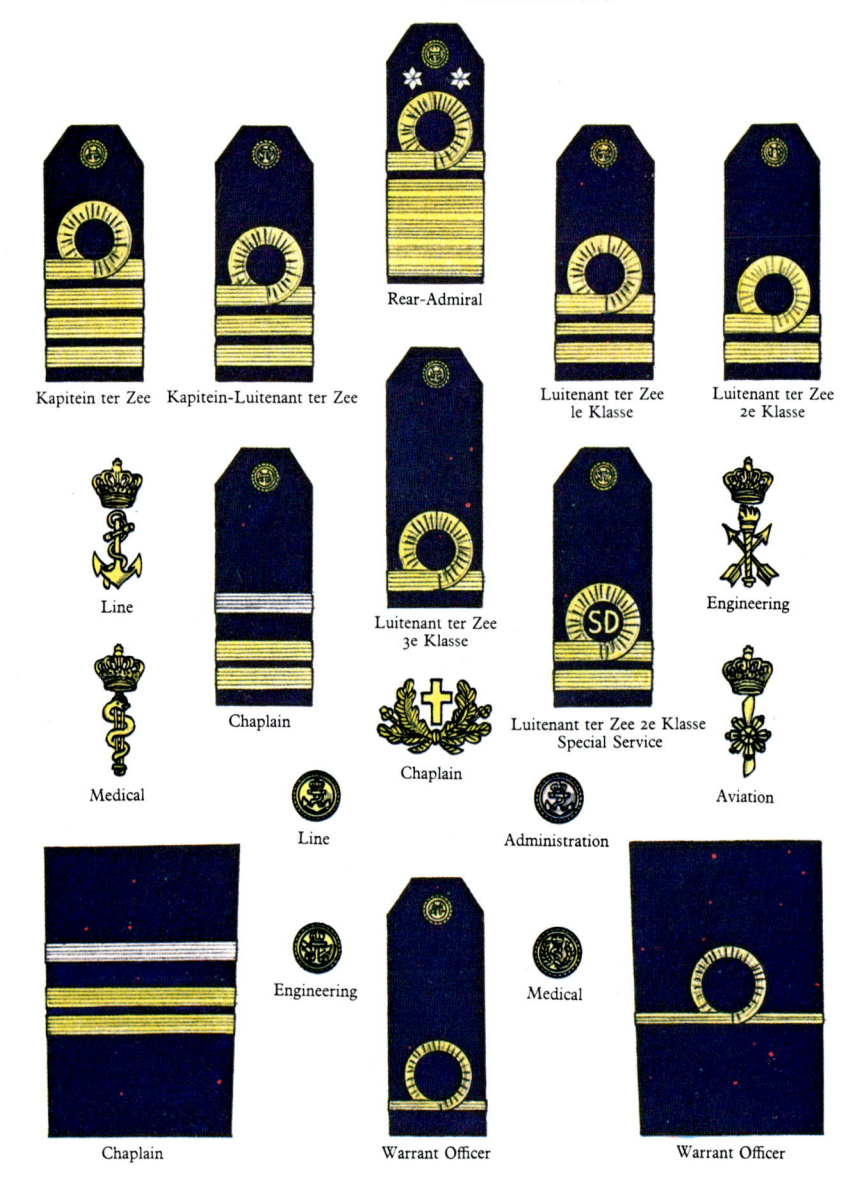

Kapitein ter Zee   Kapitein-Luitenant ter Zee   Rear-Admiral   Luitenant ter Zee 1e Klasse   Luitenant ter Zee 2e Klasse

Line

Medical

Chaplain

Luitenant ter Zee 3e Klasse

Chaplain

Luitenant ter Zee 2e Klasse Special Service

Engineering

Aviation

Line

Administration

Chaplain

Engineering

Medical

Warrant Officer

Warrant Officer

PLATE 64

NETHERLANDS

RATINGS' INSIGNIA

Chief Petty Officer

Petty Officer 1st Class

Leading Seaman
White for Yeoman Leading Seaman

WARRANT OFFICERS' AND PETTY OFFICERS' SPECIALITY BADGES

Boatswain

Ordnance Repairman

Signalman

Fire Controlman

Electrician

Nurse

Machinist

Telegraphist

Torpedoman

Aviation Repairman

Pilot

Musician

Steward, Cook

Yeoman

Storekeeper

Carpenter

KONINKLIJKE MARINE

Cap Tally

PLATE 65

NETHERLANDS

SPECIALITY AND TRADE BADGES

Signalman Leading & Seaman 1st Class

Boatswain Leading Seaman

Boatswain Seaman 1st Class

Boatswain Seaman 2nd Class

Telegraphist Leading & Seaman 1st Class

Apprentice Torpedoman 3rd year

Aviation Repairman Leading & Seaman 1st Class

Electrician Leading & Seaman 1st Class

Apprentice Carpenter 1st Class

Apprentice Fire Controlman 2nd year

Machinist Leading Seaman

Fireman Leading Seaman

Fireman – Oiler

Fireman 1st Class

Fireman 2nd Class

Pilot Leading & Seaman 1st Class Apprentice

Yeoman, Steward, Cook Seaman 1st Class

Ordnance Repairman Leading & Seaman 1st Class

Barber, Shoemaker, Tailor Seaman 1st Class

Nurse Leading & Seaman 1st Class

Storekeeper Leading & Seaman 1st Class

Musician Leading Seaman

Musician Aspirant

Musician Apprentice

Mineman

Submarine Torpedoman

Sharpshooter Rifle

Destroyer Torpedoman

Range Finder Operator

Master Diver 1st Class

Master Diver 2nd Class

Gun Captain

Diver 1st Class

Diver 2nd Class

PLATE 66

FINLAND

CAP AND RANK INSIGNIA

Officers' Badge

Officers' and P.O.s' Badge

Flag Officers   Senior Officers

Vice-Admiral

Vice-Admiral

Admiral

Rear-Admiral

Kommodori

Kommodori

Komentaja

Kapteeniluutnantti

Komentajakapteeni

Kapteniluutnantti

PLATE 67

FINLAND

CAP AND RANK INSIGNIA

Luutnantti

Aliluutnantti

Reservialiluutnantti
Reserve

Pastori
Chaplain

Shoulder Tab
Officers

Kapteeniluutnantti
Sotilasvirkamies – Specialist

Shoulder Tab
Specialists

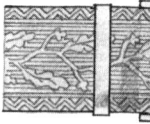

Luutnantti
Doctor

Flag Officers' Dress Belt

Officers

Specialists

Aliluutnantti
Musician

PLATE 68

FINLAND

CADETS' CAP AND RANK INSIGNIA

Navy Cadets

Cap Badge

Coast Artillery Cadets

Naval Academy Cadet

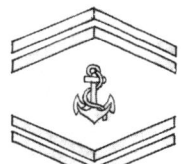

Junior Sergeant Cadet
2nd year course – Navy

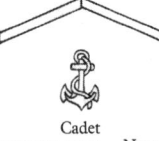

Cadet
1st year course – Navy

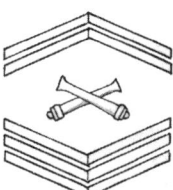

Sergeant Cadet
2nd year course – C.A.

Naval Academy
(Coast Artillery) Cadet

MERISOTAKOULU

Master Navigator
Helmsman

Candidate

Cadet

Supply Master
Supplyman

Mine Master
Mineman

Master Nurse
Nurse

WARRANT OFFICERS' RANK INSIGNIA

W.O. 1st Class
Master Machinists

W.O. 2nd Class
Torpedo Master

W.O. 3rd Class
Master Signaller

PLATE 69

FINLAND

WARRANT OFFICERS' AND PETTY OFFICERS' INSIGNIA

Master Radioman / Radio Operator

Rifleman

W.O.s' Cap Badge

Master Electrician / Electrician

Band Master / Bandsman

P.O.s' Cap Badge

Master of Ordnance

Specialist P.O.s 'Cap Badge

PETTY OFFICERS' RATE INSIGNIA

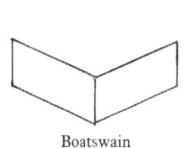

Boatswain Specialist

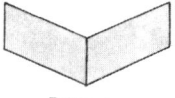

Boatswain

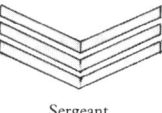

Sergeant

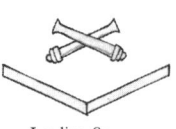

Leading Seaman Gunner

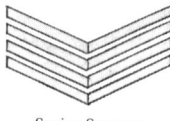

Senior Sergeant

Junior Sergeant

Junior Sergeant Conscript Radio Operator

Seaman 1st Class

Seaman 2nd Class

Seaman 3rd Class

Leading Seaman Conscript Signalman

RANNIKKOLAIVASTO

Seaman's Cap Insignia

PLATE 70

one sovereign could use the cypher of each sovereign under whom he had served.

The Honorary Chaplain to the King wore a special bronze badge, consisting of the Royal Cypher within an oval wreath, on the left side of the scarf in the conduct of religious services and on academic or ordinary clerical dress in other circumstances. A chaplain who had ceased to hold the appointment could still wear the special red cassock, but not the badge.

The chaplains' uniforms differed considerably from those of the naval officers, especially before the war, but the only relevant badges were the black Maltese crosses worn on the collar of the white tunic.

There were basically two types of buttons: flag officers and the Commodore 1st Class had a gilt raised button with a rope rim encircling a plain rim, within which was a wreath of laurel surrounding a foul anchor ensigned by the crown; the button of the other officers was the same but without the wreath. Both were made in three sizes: 37, 30 and 26 lines in button-maker's measures. Bronze buttons were used on the khaki uniform.

Cap badges for ratings, namely chief petty officers, were introduced in 1879, although engine room artificers had had the crown and anchor device since 1868. Seamen chief petty officers wore a gold and silver crown above a silver anchor, the latter in a gold ring, non-seamen had the whole badge in gold and the engine room artificers had a purple backing to the anchor, while that of the others was always black. In 1918, gold and silver badges were adopted for all.

The senior petty officers were allowed to wear peaked caps and jackets in 1920 and thus took on the badge previously used by the chief petty officers; the latter had a small gold laurel wreath added to theirs. The ring around the anchor was purely ornamental, often consisting of two cords, until, in 1970, a new order established that the Fleet Chief Petty Officer would wear two gold rings and the others one ring only.

The red cap badges for junior ratings originated in 1890, when the junior rates of many of the non-seamen branches obtained cap badges like those of the chief petty officers but embroidered in red.

There were cap badges embroidered in gold and silver, red thread, made of brass or painted red, as illustrated.

Plates 1, 2. R.N. Officers' Rank Insignia

The principal naval rank insignia consisted of rows of gold lace on the cuffs with the uppermost stripe curled into a circle.

Admirals and commodores were distinguished by a large lace stripe, $1\frac{3}{4}$ in

(44.5 mm) in width, with from one to four $\frac{9}{16}$ in (14 mm) stripes above it, the uppermost with a curl 2 in (51 mm) in diameter.

The Rear-Admiral and Commodore 1st Class had the same rows, with one large and one narrow stripe. The Commodore 2nd Class had the curl, $1\frac{3}{4}$ in (44.5 mm) in diameter, immediately above the large stripe.

The other officers used the $\frac{9}{16}$ in (14 mm) stripes, except for the Lieutenant-Commander who wore an additional $\frac{1}{4}$ in (6.5 mm) wide stripe in combination with two larger ones, as illustrated, all with the $1\frac{3}{4}$ in (44.5 mm) curl on top.

The Warrant Officer wore the narrowest stripe with curl as above. The space between the two rows of lace was $\frac{1}{4}$ in (6.5 mm) wide.

Only a few representative cuffs have been illustrated in order to save room whereas all the shoulder straps for each individual rank are shown because these are considerably smaller.

Shoulder straps were worn with greatcoat, watchcoat, white tunic and white mess jacket. All were made of blue cloth, except those of engineer, medical and accountant officers of flag rank, which were made of appropriate distinction cloth, with gold lace on top and a leather backing. The flag officers and the Commodore 1st Class had 2 in (51 mm) wide lace sewn along the shoulder straps, thus leaving a narrow piping of blue or other coloured distinction cloth exposed all around.

The shoulder straps were $5\frac{1}{4}$ in (133 mm) long and $2\frac{1}{4}$ in (57 mm) wide and had a button at the top and a leather tongue at the back.

Silver rank devices were placed on the gold lace as follows:

Rank	Devices
Admiral of the Fleet	The crown, the Royal Cypher and crossed batons surrounded by a wreath of laurel
Admiral	The crown, crossed sword and baton and three 8-pointed stars $1\frac{1}{4}$ in (32 mm) in diameter
Vice-Admiral	As above with two stars
Rear-Admiral	As above with one star $1\frac{3}{4}$ in (44.5 mm) in diameter
Commodore 1st Class	The crown, two small stars and an anchor with chain cable below

All the other officers and the Warrant Officer wore the stripes and curl, as on the cuffs, across their shoulder straps.

Executive officers had the stripes sewn directly onto cuffs and shoulder straps while non-executive officers were distinguished by a stripe, or stripes, of distinction cloth in conjuction with the rows of lace, i.e. the distinction cloth was used as backing to the stripes, below the single stripe, or on its own as a $\frac{1}{8}$ in (3 mm) wide stripe in the case of midshipmen and cadets entitled to wear distinction cloth.

The following colours of distinction cloth were used:

Branch	Distinction Cloth
Engineer Officers	Purple
Medical Officers	Scarlet
Dental Officers	Orange
Accountant Officers	White
Instructor Officers / Schoolmasters	Light blue
Shipwright Officers	Silver-grey
Wardmasters	Maroon
Electrical Officers	Dark green
Ordnance Officers	Dark blue

When serving afloat, Assistant Constructors of the Royal Corps of Naval Constructors and Electrical Engineering Officers wore the uniform prescribed for a lieutenant, the former with silver-grey distinction cloth, the latter with dark green distinction cloth between their stripes.

Khaki uniform could be worn, when ordered by the senior officer, instead of blue or white uniform, by officers employed ashore outside Great Britain; in this case stripes were displayed on the cuffs and distinction cloth, if necessary, as on the blue jacket, but gold lace was replaced by khaki braid of the same width. Blue shoulder straps with gold lace stripes were used with khaki battledress during the war.

Midshipmen of the Royal Navy wore, on each side of the collar, a white turnback of 2 in (51 mm) with a notched hole of white twist 1½ in (38 mm) long and a corresponding button, while the cadets had the notched hole and button only.

Plate 3. R.N.R. Officers' Rank Insignia

The Royal Naval Reserve was formed in 1859 and its cadre of officers was organised five years later. The latter wore the same uniforms as the officers of the Royal Navy but different insignia, which has undergone several changes and modifications since those early days. Their cap badges carried the initials 'RNR' above the anchor and waved gold braid stripes, until World War I when ordinary naval officers' cap badges were adopted and gold lace substituted for gold braid.

The stripes were one-half the width of those prescribed for officers of the Royal Navy, adapted in pairs to form two waved lines, one superimposed upon the other so that a section of blue cloth showed between the curves. A 6-pointed star, made of intersecting lace, replaced the curl.

The Commodore 2nd Class wore the large stripe straight and the Lieutenant-Commander wore the thin stripe straight but in combination with two pairs of waved stripes. The coloured cloth worn by non-executive officers did not fill the space between the two rows of lace but consisted of a narrow stripe only.

Midshipmen of the Royal Naval Reserve wore blue turnbacks and notched holes and the cadets blue notched holes on both sides of the collar.

Ratings used uniforms of the Royal Navy and the badges they were eligible to wear plus, since 1924, the initials 'RNR' on the left cuff.

Plate 4. R.N.V.R. Officers' Rank Insignia

The Royal Naval Volunteer Reserve was instituted in 1903 and its officers had the initials 'RNV' in the cap badge above the anchor and waved stripes of gold braid. As with the Royal Naval Reserve, the initials were abolished and gold lace replaced gold braid.

The waved stripes, $\frac{3}{8}$ in (9.5 mm) wide, were worn parallel to each other and surmounted by a squarish, waved curl; the Commodore 2nd Class had his large stripe set straight below the curl and the Lieutenant-Commander wore a straight $\frac{1}{8}$ in (3.2 mm) stripe between two waved ones.

Distinction cloth was placed in between the stripes; officers of the Special Branch wore distinction cloth of emerald green. By Admiralty order at 6 August 1942 the half stripe of the Lieutenant-Commander was to be waved instead of straight; by order on 6 May 1943 the half stripe on his shoulder straps was to be waved in the same way as the broad stripes.

Midshipmen and cadets of the Royal Naval Volunteer Reserve wore maroon turnbacks and notched holes of maroon twist. Chaplains, when officiating at naval, military and air force services, could wear the scarf authorised to be worn by chaplains of the Royal Navy with the addition of the letters 'RNVR' in gold, below the badge.

Ratings wore the above initials on the left cuff. In 1958 the Royal Naval Reserve and the Royal Naval Volunteer Reserve were amalgamated and the resulting organisation took over the title of the former.

Plate 5. R.N. Branch Officers' Rank Insignia

The civil branches of the Royal Navy have been mentioned already, in the introduction to this chapter and in the section dealing with officers' rank insignia.

The badges of the Fleet Air Arm have been dealt with in a previous volume dedicated to aviation insignia of World War 2. Only two examples have been illustrated in this plate: the gold and silver winged badge worn on the left forearm by naval pilots and the initial 'A', placed in the curl of the rank insignia, which identified personnel of the Air Branch.

Women's Royal Naval Service

The Women's Royal Naval Service was formed in November 1917 and its personnel became known as 'Wrens' because of the service's initials.

The organisation was disbanded after World War 1 and reformed in 1939 under the command of Mrs (afterwards Dame) Vera Laughton Mathews, who had the title of Director and initially wore four blue stripes on the cuffs, later the stripes equivalent to the male rank of Rear-Admiral. The first officers' ranks were given as Chief Officer, 1st Officer and 2nd Officer, the Superintendents having been separately recruited; 3rd Officers were appointed and in uniform by January 1940 and appeared in the Navy List for the first time in March 1940. The following were the officers' ranks of the W.R.N.S. compared with those of the Royal Navy:

W.R.N.S.	R.N.
Chief Commandant / Director W.R.N.S.	both equivalent to Rear-Admiral
Deputy Director	Commodore
Superintendent	Captain
Chief Officer	Commander
1st Officer	Lieutenant-Commander
2nd Officer	Lieutenant
3rd Officer	Sub-Lieutenant
Cadet (O.T.C. only)	Midshipman/Cadet R.N.

Chief Wrens were equivalent to Chief Petty Officer and wore the buttons on the cuffs, the rank of Petty Officer was adopted a little later in 1939 and was identified by blue crossed anchors on the left upper sleeve and the Leading Wren had a single blue anchor on the left sleeve.

The officers wore special cap badges on the tricorne hat; they were smaller than the male's badge and the 6-leaved wreath was embroidered in blue silk. Chiefs and petty officers used the tricorne hat also, with badges similar to their male counterparts but made of blue embroidery. Initially all ratings were issued with pull-on hats which were recalled in late 1942 and substituted by tricorne hats or round hats, according to rate.

The officers wore special blue stripes on the cuffs and shoulder straps, with a diamond in place of the curl. The large stripe of Chief Commandant and Director was $1\frac{3}{4}$ in (44.5 mm) in width, the normal, medium-sized stripe was $\frac{1}{2}$ in (12.7 mm) and the additional narrow stripe of the 1st Officer was $\frac{1}{4}$ in (6.3 mm) in width.

At the outbreak of the war, Dr A. Genevieve Rewcastle was appointed to W.R.N.S. Headquarters as Surgeon & Agent and, in the early 1940s, she became W.R.N.S. Medical Superintendent, wearing the normal blue rank stripes on red distinction cloth. Later, however, she was entered as a Naval

Surgeon Lieutenant (on an equal footing with the male officers), wearing a Wrens' suit and tricorne hat, but with R.N.V.R. gold waved stripes on a red backing, and a gold Royal Navy cap badge. In due course she was promoted to Surgeon Lieutenant-Commander and was transferred from the staff of the Director W.R.N.S. to that of the Medical Director-General. Other women doctors were also entered as R.N.V.R. medical officers.

Shoulder straps with rank insignia were worn on the greatcoat and on tropical rig.

Wrens wore blue non-substantive badges, without additional crowns and stars, on all uniforms. The following were used during World War 2:

6-pointed star with:

G in centre (Wrens only)	General duties: Net Defence, Boat's Crew, Laundrymaid, Messenger, Hall Porter, Postman, Steward (General) including Petty Officers' Messman and Night Porter
MT in centre	Despatch Rider, Motor Driver
C in centre	Cook
OC in centre	Officers' Cook
OS in centre	Officers' Steward, Wine Steward, Mess Caterer, Ward Room Attendant
W in centre	Writer, Mail Clerk, Degaussing Recorder, Chart and Book Corrector
Crossed flags	Communications: Visual Signaller, Coder, Teleprinter Operator, Radio-Telegraph Operator, Signal Distributing Office Watchkeeper, Switchboard Operator, Classifier
Winged lightning flash	Radar Operator (worn below crown by Chief Wrens entered before April 1942)
Dividers	Plotter, Bomb Range Marker, Chart Corrector
Crown:	
Within laurel wreath	Regulating Chief Wren
Without addition	Regulating P.O. Wren

Plates 6, 7, 8. Petty Officers' and Non-substantive Badges

The first rate badges were adopted in 1827 in the form of an anchor surmounted by the crown and an anchor alone for 1st Class and 2nd Class Petty Officers, respectively. These badges were cut out from white cloth and were sewn on the upper left sleeve.

Later the rates of Chief Petty Officer and Leading Seaman were added and the badges were changed as follows:

Chief Petty Officer	Crown and anchor surrounded by wreath
1st Petty Officer	Crown and crossed anchors
2nd Petty Officer	Crown and anchor
Leading Seaman	Anchor

The first non-substantive badge, for gunners, was introduced in 1860. Others followed and many developments and changes became necessary in order to avoid confusion between rate and speciality. In 1879 the chief petty officers obtained new uniforms, similar to those of the officers, with their own badge on the peaked cap which, as mentioned earlier, was changed in 1920 when senior petty officers were allowed to wear peaked caps as well.

By the outbreak of World War 2, the Chief Petty Officer was identified by his cap badge with wreath, three buttons on the cuffs and non-substantive badges on the collar of the jacket. The petty officers' rates were unified in 1913, when that of 2nd Class Petty Officer was abolished, but the crown and crossed anchors badge was retained and the Leading Seaman continued to wear the anchor.

Rate and non-substantive badges were red for wearing on blue uniforms, blue for white uniforms and embroidered in gold for the No. 1 uniform. Chief petty officers wore gold badges on the right forearm of the white tunic, above the three buttons.

The non-substantive badges were worn on the upper right sleeve end and consisted of a speciality device, combined or not with the crown, 6-pointed stars and letters of the alphabet. Since their introduction these badges have been constantly modified in accordance with technological developments; herewith follows a list of those used during World War 2:

Crossed guns/single gun:

Crossed—crown above, star below	Gunner's Mate
Crossed—star above, star below	Director Layer
Crossed—star above	Gunlayer (1935–39)
Crossed—star above, star and A below	Anti-aircraft Rating 1st Class
Crossed—star above, star and C below	Control Rating 1st Class
Crossed—star above, star and L below	Layer Rating 1st Class
Crossed—star above, star and P below	Patrol Service Gunnery Instructor
Crossed—star above, star and Q below	Quarters Rating 1st Class
Crossed—star above, star and R below	Radar Control Rating 1st Class
Crossed—star above, A below	Anti-aircraft Rating 2nd Class

Crossed—star above, C below	Control Rating 2nd Class
Crossed—star above, L below	Layer Rating 2nd Class
Crossed—star above, P below	Patrol Service Gunlayer
Crossed—star above, Q Below	Quarters Rating 2nd Class
Crossed—star above, R Below	Radar Control Rating 2nd Class
Crossed—star above, Q and DEMS below	Gunlayer, Defensively Equipped Merchant Ships
Crossed—BD below	Gunlayer, Boom Defence
Single—star above	C.P.O. Gunner
Single—star above, A below	Anti-aircraft Rating 3rd Class
Single—star above, C below	Control Rating 3rd Class
Single—star above, L below	Layer Rating 3rd Class
Single—star above, P below	Seaman Gunner Patrol Service
Single—star above, Q below	Quarters Rating 3rd Class
Single—star above, R below	Radar Control Rating 3rd Class
Single—star above, Q and DEMS below	Seaman Gunner, Defensively Equipped Merchant Ships
Single—BD below	Quarters Rating 3rd Class, Boom Defence

The gun was the first device to be adopted in 1860 and, at that time, looked like an old cannon; the modern version came into use in 1903. Since then, and after World War 2, many other badges not mentioned in this context have been used, starting with those depicting crossed guns or the single gun, both with crown and star above and one star below, and many others with different letters of the alphabet. In general, the use of letters became widespread during the war; before, they were rarely used to identify a specific trade or a service, such is the case of the 'SSS' which stands for Shore Signal Service.

The torpedo, initially crossed with a cannon, appeared in 1885 and on its own in 1903, in two versions: the crossed torpedoes and single torpedo badge, as follows:

Crossed torpedoes/Single torpedo:

Crossed—crown above, star below	Torpedo Gunner's Mate
Crossed—crown above, wheel below	Torpedo Coxwain
Crossed—star above, star below	Leading Torpedoman (Low Power)
Crossed—star above	Leading Torpedoman
Crossed—star above, star and CM below	P.O., Controlled Mining
Crossed—star above, star and CMS below	P.O., Observation Mining
Crossed—star above, star and MS below	P.O., Wireman, Minesweeping

Crossed—star above, star and LC below	P.O., Wireman, Landing Craft
Crossed—star above, star and J below	P.O., Wireman, Cable Jointing
Crossed—star above, star and L below	P.O., Wireman
Crossed—star above, CM below	Leading Wireman, Controlled Mining
Crossed—star above, star and CMS below	Leading Wireman, Observation Mining
Crossed—star above, MS below	Leading Wireman, Minesweeping
Crossed—star above, LC below	Leading Wireman, Landing Craft
Crossed—star above, J below	Leading Wireman, Cable Jointing
Crossed—star above, L below	Leading Wireman
Single—star above	Seaman Torpedoman (1904–47), C.P.O. Torpedoman (1909–47)
Single—star above, CM below	Wireman, Controlled Mining
Single—star above, CMS below	Wireman, Observation Mining
Single—star above, MS below	Wireman, Minesweeping
Single—star above, LC below	Wireman, Landing Craft
Single—CM below	Watchkeeper, Controlled Mining
Single—BD below	Torpedo Rating, Boom Defence

Torpedo ratings, besides dealing with torpedoes, handled highly specialised electrical tasks; wiremen installed and maintained electrical equipment.

The crossed signalling flags and the ship's propeller were introduced in 1890. the highest rating of the former was the Chief Yeoman of Signals, who wore crown and star above and two stars below the crossed flags from 1909 to 1932.

Crossed flags:

Crown above, star below	Visual Signalman 1st Class
Crown above	Visual Signalman 2nd Class (C.P.O. and P.O.)
Crown above, SSS below	P.O., R.N. Shore Signal Service
Star above, two stars below	Visual Signalman 2nd Class (if below P.O.)
Star above, star below	Visual Signalman 3rd Class
Star above	Trained Operator (Visual Signalling)
Without addition	Signalman if not trained operator (Visual Signalling)
SSS below	Signalman, R.N. Shore Signal Service

BD below	Visual Signalman (Boom Defence)
LC below	Landing Craft Signalman
Star above, C below	Leading Coder (1940–41)
C below	Leading Coder (1941–48), Coder (1940–48)

3-bladed propeller:

Crown and star above, star below	Chief Motor Mechanic
Crown above, star below	Mechanician
Crown above	Stoker P.O.
Star above, star below	Motor Mechanic
Star above	Leading Stoker, Stoker 1st Class
Without addition	Stoker 2nd Class
FF below	Stoker, Fire-fighter

2-bladed propeller:

Crown and star above, star below	Chief Motor Mechanic
Star above, star below	Motor Mechanic

The 2-bladed propeller above differed from that used by ratings of naval aviation as the former was a ship's propeller while the latter was an aircraft's propeller.

Badges for wireless telegraphists were adopted in 1909 and the following were used during World War 2:

Winged lightning flash:

Crown above, star below	Wireless Telegraphist 1st Class
Crown above	Wireless Telegraphist 2nd Class if C.P.O., P.O.
Star above, two stars below	Wireless Telegraphist 2nd Class, if not C.P.O., P.O.
Star above, star below	Wireless Telegraphist 3rd Class
Star above	Wireless Telegraphist, Trained Operator
Without addition	Telegraphist, not Trained Operator
Crown and A above, M below	Radio Mechanic, Fleet Air Arm, if C.P.O.
Crown above, M below	Qualified Radio Mechanic, if C.P.O.
A above, M below	Radio Mechanic, Fleet Air Arm, if not C.P.O.
M below	Radio Mechanic
P below	Radar Plot Rating
R below	Radar Control Rating

Crown above, SWS below	P.O., Shore Wireless Service
SWS below	Telegraphist, Shore Wireless Service

The Shore Wireless Service, like the Shore Signal Service previously mentioned was a pre-war organisation; the other letters, 'A', 'M', 'P' and 'R' were introduced in 1944.

The red cross for sick berth ratings was adopted in 1885 and developed in the following badges by the early 1940s:

Red cross:

D above	Dental Surgery Attendant
DM above	Dental Mechanic
L above	Laboratory Attendant
M above	Masseur
O above	Operating Room Assistant
X above	X-ray Assistant
Without addition	Sick Berth Attendant

Crowns, stars and letters below the device were added after World War 2; earlier all ratings up to Chief Petty Officer used the same badge.

Crossed clubs:

Crown above, star below	Physical and Recreational Training Instructor 1st Class
Crown above	Physical and Recreational Training Instructor 2nd Class

Crossed axe and hammer:

Crown above	Chief Shipwright
Star above	Chief Blacksmith, Chief Plumber, Chief Painter, Chief Cooper
Without addition	All other Artisans

Gun over crossed axe and hammer:

Star above	Chief Armourer
Without addition	Armourer's Mate and Crew

Coil of rope below harpoon crossed with lightning:

Crown above	Submarine Detector Instructor
Star above, star below	Higher Submarine Detector
Without addition	Submarine Detector
Star above, star and S below	Harbour Defence Operator 1st Class
Star above, S below	Harbour Defence Operator 2nd Class

S below	Harbour Defence Operator 3rd Class

Crossed fid and marline spike:
Star above	Chief Sailmaker, Sailmaker
Without addition	Sailmaker's Mate, Fabric Worker

Crossed shackle and marline spike:
Star above, BD below	Chief Rigger, Rigger, Boom Defence
BD below	Rigger's Mate, Boom Defence

Cobweb and lightning flashes:
Crown above, star below	Radar Plot Instructor
Star above, star below	Radar Plot Rating 1st Class
Star above	Radar Plot Rating 2nd Class
Without addition	Radar Plot Rating 3rd Class

Dividers:
Without addition	Navigator's Yeoman

Camera:
Crown above	C.P.O. and P.O. Photographer
Star above	Leading Photographer
Without addition	Photographer

A new set of non-substantive badges, depicting a 6-pointed star with an initial in its centre, was introduced in 1932 and used until 1948. Later, others were added, with different letters, and crowns and stars were added to the basic devices for petty officers' rates.

6-pointed star with:
C in centre	Cook
OC in centre	Officers' Cook
OS in centre	Officers' Steward
S in centre	Supply Rating
W in centre	Writer

The officers' cooks and stewards wore plain 'OC' or 'OS' as a badge during World War 1.

Rangefinder:
Star above, star below	Rangetaker 1st Class

Sextant:
Without addition	Surveying Recorder

A set of four aviation badges appeared in 1935. The device was an aeroplane with straight wings which, in 1939, was changed to an aeroplane with swept wings and, in the same year, aviation mechanics and fitters obtained badges displaying propellers, as follows:

Aeroplane:

Crown above, star below	Rating Observer
Crown above	Acting Rating Observer
Star above, star below	Air Gunner 1st Class
Star above	Air Gunner 2nd Class
Without addition	Air Gunner 3rd Class, Naval Airman, General Duties

2-bladed aircraft propeller:

Crown above, A below	Air Mechanic (Airframes), C.P.O. and P.O.
Star above, A below	Air Mechanic (Airframes), Leading Rating
A below	Air Mechanic (Airframes), Other Ratings
Crown above, E below	Air Mechanic (Engines), C.P.O. and P.O.
Star above, E below	Air Mechanic (Engines), Leading Rating
E below	Air Mechanic (Engines), Other Ratings
Crown above, L below	Air Mechanic (Electrical), C.P.O. and P.O.
Star above, L below	Air Mechanic (Electrical), Leading Rating
L below	Air Mechanic (Electrical), Other Ratings
Crown above, O below	Air Mechanic (Ordnance), C.P.O. and P.O.
Star above, O below	Air Mechanic (Ordnance), Leading Rating
O below	Air Mechanic (Ordnance), Other Ratings
Without addition	Air Mechanic, Unclassified

4-bladed aircraft propeller:

Star above, A below	Air Fitter (Airframes), Leading Rating and above

A below	Air Fitter (Airframes) below Leading Rating
Star above, E below	Air Fitter (Engines) Leading Rating and above
E below	Air Fitter (Engines) below Leading Rating
Star above, L below	Air Fitter (Electrical) Leading Rating
L below	Air Fitter (Electrical) below Leading Rating
Star above, O below	Air Fitter (Ordnance) Leading Rating and above
O below	Air Fitter (Ordnance) below Leading Rating
Without addition	Air Fitter, Unclassified
Crown:	
Within laurel wreath	Master-at-Arms, C.P.O.
Without addition	Regulating P.O.
Crossed rifles:	
Without addition	Marksman
Diver's helmet:	
Without addition	Diver
Bugle:	
Without addition	Bugler
Bomb:	
Without addition	Bomb Disposal

The badge of Combined Operations was worn by personnel of the Royal Navy and of the Royal Marines, on a round background by the latter; it was worn on the right cuff of the naval ratings' uniform and on both upper sleeves of the khaki battledress. The last four badges listed were worn on the right cuff, with the exception of the Chief Petty Officer Diver, who wore the badge in the usual manner.

Rate and career in a speciality were unrelated and each speciality developed its own badges; therefore the crowns and stars on the badges of one speciality did not necessarily have the same meaning as they had in another. Many new badges appeared in the 1930s and 1940s until, eventually, in 1948, a process of reorganisation began with the aim of establishing some order among the non-substantive badges.

Only a few examples of these have been illustrated; however, at least one of each speciality listed is included.

Good conduct chevrons were adopted in 1849 for wearing on the left upper sleeve, on their own or under rate insignia of Petty Officer and below. There were gold, red and blue stripes according to uniform: one stripe for three years' service, two for eight and three for thirteen or more years of good service.

Plate 8. Cap Tallies

In peace-time the cap ribbon, or tally, identified the ship or establishment to which a sailor belonged, while during the war it displayed the initials 'H.M.S.' only, standing for 'His Majesty's Ship'.

The Commonwealth nations followed the same principal; thus, in wartime, their sailors displayed the initials 'H.M.S.' combined with national initials, except for the South Africans who had the initials 'S.A.' with a crowned anchor in the middle.

The uniforms and insignia of the Royal Navy were used throughout the Commonwealth, but buttons were different: the Canadians and Australians had their country's name across the centre and below the anchor, respectively; the buttons of the Indian Navy carried the Star of India as a background to the usual crowned anchor, and the South Africans buttons displayed the initials 'S.A.' and the crowned anchor, as on the tally.

The tallies were black with gold wire, later with yellow silk letters woven in the centre; the tally's ends were tied into a bow which naval regulations prescribed to be worn above the left ear while often the bow was worn, unofficially, above the left eye instead, and with a silver $3d$. piece placed into its centre in order to improve its appearance.

The five examples of ship's tallies illustrated were all worn by Stanley A. Statham, formerly Leading Torpedoman (Low Power). H.M.S. *Glorious* was an aircraft carrier, *Cossack* was a Tribal class destroyer, *Effingham* was a cruiser of the Hawkins Class, which was lost in 1940, *Neptune*, a one-stack cruiser of the Leander Class, lost in 1941.

The badge of the Royal Navy Youth Entries was worn on the upper sleeve of the uniform by Sea Cadets or personnel of the Home Guard and Air Training Corps and identified young men, aged 17 years, accepted by the navy and awaiting call-up at the age of 18 years.

Plate 9. Merchant Navy, Royal National Lifeboat Institution and H.M. Coastguard

A small number of insignia of these three organisations have been illustrated in order to prevent the reader from confusing them with those of the Royal

Navy. There were others as well because several steamships' companies had their own uniforms and badges.

The officers of the Merchant Navy displayed special rank insignia, i.e. stripes of gold lace combined with a diamond, and had special rank titles, which differed according to speciality. The Captain (Certified Master) wore four stripes, the two middle ones joined to form a diamond, the Chief Officer, 1st Officer, 2nd Officer and 3rd Officer wore respectively three stripes, two and a narrower stripe, two stripes and one stripe, all combined with the diamond. The uncertified Junior Officer had one stripe only, with a half diamond, i.e. the stripe was twisted to form a 'v' in the centre of the cuff.

Distinction cloth was displayed as illustrated, red for Surgeon, purple for Engineer and white for Purser.

The wireless officers wore waved stripes: the 1st Wireless Officer had two stripes and the diamond, while the 2nd and 3rd had two stripes and one respectively, without the diamond. Stewards were identified by one straight stripe below 6-pointed gold stars.

The officers of H.M. Coastguard wore from one to four stripes with curl on the cuffs; the Chief Inspector had the two outer stripes of gold lace and his deputy of silver, while all other stripes were made of black lace.

The Inspectors and Higher Grades and the District Officers wore the cap badge with oak wreath and had the visor of the peaked cap covered with blue cloth. Inspectors and Higher Grades had black oak leaves embroidered along the edge of the visor, the District Officers had a plain blue cloth visor and the others wore the smaller cap badge and black leather visor.

The Coxswain of the Royal National Lifeboat Institution was distinguished from the other ratings by his cap badge alone.

The Royal Marines

The Royal Marines trace their origins to the Duke of York and Albany's Maritime Regiment of Foot, otherwise known as the Admiral's Regiment, formed in 1664, and recruited largely from the Trained Bands of London. They were organised into a permanent corps in 1775, with 'Divisions' at Chatham, Portsmouth and Plymouth, under the control of the Board of Admiralty.

The Royal Marines provided detachments of small-arms men for duty on the upper decks of His Majesty's ships and landing parties, and in these roles they helped to protect and consolidate the empire for centuries.

During the French Wars they were present at every naval battle; nearly three thousand officers and men were at Trafalgar, whilst they also gained much experience and distinction in innumerable raiding and other amphibious operations. They were rewarded by the granting of the title 'Royal' in 1802.

Artillery companies were added to the Corps in 1804 to man a portion of the armament of the ship and, as their role in defence of ships subsided, they were redeployed in land operations; thus, after the Crimean War, they were divided into Blue Marines (Royal Marine Artillery) and Red Marines (Royal Marine Light Infantry).

These two branches were amalgamated in 1923 under the old title the Royal Marines.

During World War 2 they were called upon to perform a whole range of new tasks: formations for the defence of naval bases overseas, providing crews for landing crafts, beach control parties and armoured units for close support on the beaches, not to mention the well-known R.M. Commandos. All this in addition to their normal activities, such as the defence of ships, the forming of battalions, siege regiments and anti-aircraft units.

Plate 10. Badges of the Royal Marines

The badge of the Royal Marines is composed of the Royal Crest, which was initially displayed on the officers' shoulder belt plates in 1797, by the laurel wreath, which it is claimed was awarded to them after the battle of Belle-Île in 1761, and by the globe. The latter was granted by King George IV in 1827, when the Royal Marines claimed one hundred and six battle honours in campaigns all over the world for their new colours and received the globe instead.

Only one battle honour was selected for display; it commemorates the capture and defence of Gibraltar, the marines' proudest achievement. The motto *Per Mare Per Terram*, believed to have been used for the first time in 1775, means 'By Sea By Land' and truly describes their deployment. The anchor is often portrayed in the Royal Marines' Insignia to denote that the Corps is part of the Naval Service. It was first used by the marines in 1747.

The cap badges displayed the Royal Crest, the globe and the wreath; the collar badges the globe and wreath only; all were in two variants, for blue dress and khaki service dress uniforms.

The officers' dress cap badge had a silver globe with the continents above it painted in gold, the Royal Crest and wreath were made of gilt and the former was detached from the rest. The Warrant Officer and Quartermaster Sergeant also wore cap badges in two separate pieces but entirely finished in gilt. The Sergeants had gilt cap badges but in one piece, with the crest attached to the ends of the wreath and on the top of the globe; the other ranks had the same badge but made of brass.

The dress collar badges followed the pattern of the cap badge, therefore the officers' had the silver globe, those of the Warrant Officers, Quartermaster Sergeant and Sergeants were identical, i.e. made of gilt, and the collar badges of the other ranks were made of brass. Collar badges had shorter fittings at the back than cap badges.

The officers wore smaller collar badges on the lapels of the mess dress. The first badge illustrated, with the wreath joining on top, was used from 1897 to 1921; another badge, with a small bugle in between the ends of the wreath, was worn from 1921 to 1923 by officers of the Royal Marine Light Infantry and matched their cap badges, which carried the bugle instead of the Royal Crest. The other badge illustrated, with the wreath's ends parted, was used from 1923 to 1953, later followed by an anodised version.

Before the war, until 1939, a silver globe and embroidered wreath was worn by officers on the collar of the frock coat, while other ranks had collar badges embroidered in yellow thread on a red background for the collar of the blue tunic.

Bronze cap badges were worn on khaki caps and, again, there were two versions: with detached crest for officers, the Warrant Officer and Quartermaster Sergeant, and in a single piece for all other ranks. Black bakelite cap and collar badges were issued to the other ranks during World War 2.

The lyre was adopted in 1906 as a distinguishing badge for the personnel of the Naval School of Music. It was worn on cap badges in place of the Royal Crest and a vast array could be found: some badges were gilded, others made of brass with the lyre detached or attached either to the ends of the wreath or to the globe as well. The lyre was worn above the globe and laurels from 1921 to 1946 and was then replaced by the normal R.M. cap badge.

The officers wore the lyre on the collar with an additional scroll which carried the motto from 1921 to 1930, the other ranks had the plain lyre in brass or embroidered in yellow on red backing; the latter badge was abolished in 1939 when the wearing of blue dress was discontinued but the brass badge continued to be used until 1951 and by Boys Junior Musicians until 1970, later in an anodised version.

The 'RMB' titles, which come in small and large variations were also adopted in 1921; one type was made without the top bar across and has a full stop after the initials. The normal shoulder titles of the Royal Marines, with initials 'RM', were made in bronze and in brass, in small and large sizes.

The three divisional bands, at Chatham, Portsmouth and Plymouth, were granted special cap devices: the former received the silver Rose of York in 1902 as a reward for accompanying the Duke of Cornwall and York, the future King George V, on his tour of the colonies.

The band of the Portsmouth Division was granted the Prince of Wales's Plume in 1876 to commemorate the prince's visit to India and was worn until the amalgamation of the R.M.A. and R.M.L.I. in 1923. Later the badge was still worn by bandsmen at Deal until that band was dispersed in 1930. However, the band of the Royal Marine Artillery went with King George V to India for the Delhi Durbar and thus was awarded the King's Cypher on the ball of the grenade of the cap badge, a distinction which was retained by the band of the Portsmouth Division.

The Prince of Wales's Plume was also granted to the R.M.L.I. band of Plymouth in 1921 for going with the prince, later King Edward VIII, on his visit to Canada and Australia.

The band serving on the Royal Yacht, since 1925, wear a special shoulder flash which, in fact, reads 'Royal Yacht', and it is still worn today underneath an embroidered crown.

The officers wore rank insignia of army pattern, in gold or bronze according to type of uniforms, and shoulder titles.

The rank of Warrant Officer was instituted in 1943 and was identified by the initials 'WO' surrounded by a laurel wreath, as illustrated, on the shoulder straps. In April 1949 it was abolished and the warrant officers still in charge were upgraded to commissioned officers.

Other rank badges typical of the marines were those for quartermaster sergeant instructors: the Royal Crown within a laurel wreath above crossed guns for gunnery, above crossed rifles for musketry and above crossed clubs for the physical training instructors.

The Royal Marines, although a naval organisation, were basically a separate body, primarily where uniforms and insignia were concerned. The officers' rank distinction followed the army's pattern, but had a special rank of Captain-General, later taken by King George VI and at present by the Duke of Edinburgh. The non-commissioned officers used a mixture of army and navy badges, including some non-substantive badges, which worked out perfectly for their own purpose, and some extra badges of their own.

The King's Badge was adopted in March 1918, following King George V's inspection to R.M. Depot at Deal. It was granted to the best all-round marine in each King's Squad and he kept it throughout his service. At the same time the title of 'King's Squad' was given to each recruits' squad as it became in turn the senior squad in the Corps. The badge was worn on the right upper sleeve of all uniforms and therefore many variations are in existence: the Royal Cypher and surrounding laurel wreath in gold on dark blue, or red on dark blue, gold on red, gold on dark green, white on khaki or brown on summer drill background, according to uniform.

Plate 11. Badges of the Royal Marines

Formation signs were adopted during World War 2 for wearing on the upper sleeves of the battledress.

The Royal Marines Division was in existence from 1941 to 1943 and later the trident was used by the 116th R.M. Brigade, which was formed by the 27th, 28th and 30th R.M. battalions. The 117th R.M. Brigade (31st, 32nd and 33rd R.M. Bns) wore the foul anchor within an 8-pointed star in 1945.

The anchor, with a gold grenade superimposed, was used by the R.M. Engineers from 1940 to 1945 and by the personnel of the 34th Amphibian Support Regiment in 1945–46. A seahorse was the emblem of the 104th Training Brigade, which, in 1943, was redesignated R.M. Training Group.

The R.M. Siege Regiment used a grenade with protruding ball embroidered in red thread and 'T', 'U' and 'W' 4 in (102 mm) batteries of the R.M. Coast Artillery were distinguished by a small maroon triangle from 1941 to 1944.

Red figures cut out from felt and sewn on khaki background were worn on the shoulder straps during the war; an Arabic '7' was used by the 7th R.M. Battalion in 1941–42 and a Roman 'VII' in 1943–44 until March, when the battalion was converted to become the 48 R.M. Commando. The 9th R.M. Battalion used the Roman figure from 1941 until August 1943 when it became the 46 R.M. Commando. Other badges existed as well but only those of the 7th and 9th battalions are displayed at the Royal Marines Museum.

The 30th Assault Unit used the number '30', embroidered in light blue thread on a dark blue background, the 31st R.M. Battalion had a red '31' on khaki and the 33rd had a red '33' on a dark blue background. These badges were worn in the later months of the War.

The shoulder title of the Royal Marines was straight, with red lettering on a blue background, and was worn on battledress by all except commandos from 1943 to 1966. The woven pattern was issued and commandos wore it with the number above and 'COMMANDO' designation below, in three pieces attached together.

Unofficial badges were worn as well: some 'ROYAL MARINES' titles were red on ultramarine blue instead of dark blue, or with dark blue lettering on a red background. There were embroidered commandos' titles, often with the wording displaced, as for the example illustrated of a shoulder title of the 44 R.M. Commando. New curved titles were adopted by the commandos in 1946.

Royal Navy titles were curved, embroidered in white thread on a dark blue background. There were three; besides those illustrated, there was one which displayed only the designation 'COMMANDO'.

The triangular formation sign with the red dagger was used by the personnel of the Special Service Group in 1944–46 and, after the disbandment of the army commandos, it was worn by the 3rd R.M. Commando Brigade from 1946 to 1976 and later re-adopted by army personnel.

The Union of Socialist Soviet Republics

Peter the Great was the creator of the first Russian fleet and he engaged English technicians and naval officers with the purpose of extending Russian power across the seas. However, Russia was basically a land nation without direct access to the Atlantic and Mediterranean and hampered by lack of communications with its far east territories.

Eventually three main fleets developed: the Baltic Fleet, which could not get out from the Baltic Sea without the goodwill of the neighbouring countries; the Black Sea Fleet, trapped in that sea by Turkey, and the Far Eastern Fleet, based at Vladivostok, lost beyond Siberia and without much scope for deployment.

The latter was badly mauled during the Russo–Japanese War and later World War 1 and the successive Revolution obliterated the last vestiges of Russian naval power.

Slowly the fleet was reorganised, new ships were built, but not even during World War 2 was the Soviet Navy strong enough to achieve any outstanding success although, in fairness, the great battles fought by land armies on the Eastern Front minimised the valid cooperation given by the other services.

The insignia used after February 1943 are illustrated in this chapter dedicated to the Soviet Navy, as conventional naval insignia were worn previously by all ranks.

Plate 11. Cap and Rank Insignia

The officers of the Soviet Navy were divided into executive and non-executive officers: the former included those of the Line and Line Engineering, the latter the officers serving in all the other naval corps or services.

Line officers wore gold insignia, i.e. the cap badge and embroideries on the peaked cap's visor, cuff stripes, shoulder straps, buttons, etc. while the officers of the services had gold or silver insignia according to specific branch. Therefore there were gold or silver cap badges.

The badge depicted a foul anchor superimposed on a round, protruding cockade with black centre, surrounded by a laurel wreath, the whole ensigned by the 5-pointed red star with hammer and sickle in a white centre.

The flag officer's cap was fitted with a double cord and displayed two sprigs of laurel leaves on the peak, the Captains of 1st, 2nd and 3rd Rank had a black leather chin strap and one row of oak leaves on the peak. Cords and embroideries were of gold or silver, according to branch of service. Cap badges and embroideries were later made of metal, finished as an imitation of embroidery.

The flag officers' buttons depicted the emblem of the Soviet Union above crossed anchors while those of all other ranks carried the anchor alone.

Plates 12, 13. Officers' Rank Insignia

Executive and non-executive officers had different rank insignia and rank titles as the latter were designated by army titles.

They displayed rank insignia in the form of stripes below a 5-pointed star on the cuffs and by means of shoulder straps.

At the beginning of the war the officers wore conventional stripes of lace on the cuffs but new regulations published in February 1943 introduced shoulder straps of traditional Russian pattern, made of gold or silver lace according to corps, and shorter cuff stripes.

The shoulder straps were used by all officers on the dark jacket, tunic and greatcoat while cuff stripes were worn by officers of the Line and Line Engineering only. However, the officers of the other corps wore special trimmings on the cuffs of the dress jacket, in gold or silver according to the metal of their shoulder straps and with the same distinction cloth backing. Only shoulder straps were worn on the white tunic and on the greatcoat.

The cuff stripes of the service dress measured $3\frac{1}{8}$ in (80 mm) in length and those of the parade jacket $3\frac{15}{16}$ in (100 mm). The flag officers' and Captain 1st Rank's stripe was $1\frac{3}{16}$ in (30 mm) wide and the other two were $\frac{1}{2}$ in (12.7 mm) and $\frac{1}{4}$ in (6.5 mm) wide; the latter was worn combined with larger ones by the ranks of Captain-Lieutenant and Lieutenant. The stars above the stripes were embroidered in gold and measured 2 in (51 mm) in diameter for flag officers and $1\frac{3}{16}$ in (30 mm) for the other officers.

The trimmings on the cuffs of the corps officers' dress jacket identified class of rank: the generals wore three stripes and three double bars, the senior officers had two stripes and two double bars and junior officers had one stripe and one double bar only, in gold or silver according to corps.

The shoulder straps were the same as those used by the army and identified rank and branch of service. Officers of the Line and Line Engineering had gold ones with black piping and the latter were distinguished by the additional engineers' badge (crossed wrench and hammer). The flag officers (admirals) wore gold naval stars of rank on the shoulder straps while the generals of the corps had army type stars, as illustrated.

The shoulder straps of the flag officers were covered by gold or silver lace of admirals'/generals' pattern, with a zigzag design interwoven; the senior officers' gold or silver shoulder straps carried two longitudinal lines of coloured piping and those of the junior officers had one line of piping only. The button was always of the same metal as the lace while the rank stars of the generals and of the officers, and the corps badge, were made in the opposite metal, i.e. silver on gold and vice versa.

The following shoulder straps were used during the war:

Corps	Lace	Piping	Badge
Line	gold	black	—
Line Engineering	gold	black	Crossed wrench and hammer
Aviation	gold	light blue	—
Aviation Engineering	gold	light blue	Crossed wrench and hammer
Coastal Defence	gold	brown	—
Naval Constructions	silver	black	Crossed wrench and hammer
Supply	silver	red	—
Medical (with mil. training)	silver	red/green	Serpent and cup

The silver shoulder straps of the medical officers had green piping embodied and red piping around the outer edges.

The officers of auxiliary services were identified by narrow shoulder straps, $\frac{3}{16}$ in (4.5 mm) wide for a general and $\frac{5}{32}$ in (4 mm) for other officers, as admirals'/generals' shoulder straps were always slightly wider than those of the others.

The following were in existence:

Corps	Lace	Piping	Badge
Medical (without mil. training)	silver	red	Gold serpent and cup
Veterinary	silver	red	Silver serpent and cup
Administration	silver	red	—
Legal	silver	red	Shield on crossed swords

The Guards' badge was instituted on 28 March 1942 as an award for units of the armed forces which had gained particular distinction in battle. The badge was made of brass and enamel.

Plate 14. Cap and Rate Insignia

Midshipmen and chief petty officers wore uniforms of officers' type, the former with officers' cap badge and the latter with their own badge, depicting a foul anchor ensigned by the red star and surrounded by a rope. All the other ratings had sailors' uniforms with a sailors' cap with tally and red star. Petty officers with more than 5 years' service were entitled to wear the peaked cap with the red star at the front.

The black cap tallies carried the name of a fleet, for instance 'BLACK SEA FLEET' or the name of a ship's crew, for instance 'THE GLORIOUS'; the tally illustrated reads 'RED CAUCASUS'. Ratings serving on ships awarded Guards' attribute wore tallies with orange stripes, inspired by the old order of bravery of St George.

In 1943 the rate badges were transferred from the sleeves on to the shoulder straps and consisted of yellow lace stripes, as illustrated. Letters of the cyrillic alphabet were attached to the outer ends of the shoulder straps to identify the wearer's unit or organisation.

Circular trade badges were worn on the upper sleeves: the trade's devices were embroidered in red and the actual badges, of the same colour as the uniform on which they were intended to be worn, had a red edging. The Boatswain had an anchor, the Helmsman a steering wheel, the Gunner crossed guns, etc.

The leather belt of the ratings carried a brass buckle with the star and hammer and sickle within, superimposed upon an anchor.

Marines wore a gold foul anchor on the left upper sleeve and aviators wore the winged badges illustrated in previous volumes.

Denmark

The Danish Navy was founded by King Hans in 1500 and, due to the insular configuration of Denmark, the fleet played a dominant role in the history and development of the nation.

Its greatest victory was won at the battle of the Bay of Koege in 1677 against the Swedish Navy and other successful engagements took place in the Great Northern War, during the period between 1701 and 1720.

The Battle of Copenhagen is widely known because it was fought against the British fleet under the command of Admiral Nelson. The last important engagement occurred in 1864, when the Danish Navy won against a combined Austro–Prussian force.

Plate 15. Officers' Cap and Rank Insignia

The insignia worn during World War 2 followed the rules established by the regulations published in 1937 and were used until 1951 when drastic changes took place. No shoulder straps were used by the Danish Navy until 1951 and the flag officers' insignia and other badges were altered then too.

Flag officers, senior officers and junior officers wore different cap badges; all had the crown above an oval red-white-red Danish cockade with the foul anchor superimposed but the surrounding oak leaves wreath was different for each class of rank. The flag officers' wreath was somewhat larger than that of the senior officers, although both had twelve leaves, while the junior officers' wreath had ten leaves only.

Rank was identified by gold lace stripes on the cuffs. Flag officers used stripes $1\frac{1}{8}$ in (28 mm) in width, in combination with $\frac{9}{16}$ in (14 mm) stripes, with the top one twisted in a round curl.

The other executive officers wore rows of $\frac{9}{16}$ in (14 mm) lace in combination with narrower ones, with the curl; the officers of three special branches were identified by devices in the curl and the officers of the corps had stripes on distinction cloth backing, with the corps emblem in place of the curl.

The initial 'R' superimposed upon an anchor was the device for the officers of the Reserve, the initial 'F' ('Flyver') identified an officer of Aviation and 'K' ('Kyst') an officer of the Coast Artillery.

In 1951 the same cap badge was introduced for all officers, from admiral to sub-lieutenant, new flag officers' rank insignia of British pattern were adopted, together with ornaments of gold oak leaves on the peaked cap's visor.

Plate 16. Officers' Rank Insignia

The officers of the corps included naval engineers, supply officers and medical officers, who had different rank titles: 'Maskinmester', 'Intendant' and 'Laege', respectively.

The executive officers and the officers of the corps had not the same hierarchy of rank: the engineers and intendants, for instance, had an intermediate rank between Sub-Lieutenant of 1st and of 2nd Grade, in the form of one medium and one narrow gold stripe, but did not use the rank identified by two medium and two narrow stripes. The top rank they could reach was 'Stabsmaskinmester' and 'Stabsintendant', respectively, which corresponded to the executive rank of Commander-Captain.

The medical officers reached the rank of 'Stabslaege' with four medium stripes but did not use the rank corresponding to Commander-Captain, nor the intermediate rank of the engineers and intendants mentioned above.

The officers of the corps could be identified as follows:

Corps	Badge	Distinction Cloth
Naval Engineers	Anchor and propeller	Crimson
Supply	Anchor and caduceus	White
Medical	Anchor and Aesculapius staff	Poppy red

The corps badges were embroidered in gold wire. The distinction cloth was shown in between the stripes, or below a single stripe. The following is a comparative scheme of ranks:

Executive Officers	Naval Engineers	Supply Officers	Medical Officers
Commander	—	—	Staff Doctor
Commander-Captain	Staff Machinist-Master	Staff Intendant	—
Captain (two ranks)	—	—	Senior Doctor (two ranks)
	Machinist-Master 1st Grade	Senior Intendant	
Captain-Lieutenant	Machinist-Master 2nd Grade	Intendant 1st Grade	Senior Doctor 2nd Grade
Sub-Lieutenant 1st Grade	Machinist-Master 3rd Grade	Intendant 2nd Grade	Asst Doctor over 3 years service
—	Junior Machinist-Master 1st/2nd Grade over 3 years service	Asst Intendant over 3 years service	—

Executive Officers	Naval Engineers	Supply Officers	Medical Officers
Sub-Lieutenant 2nd Grade	Junior Machinist-Master 2nd Grade under 3 years service	Asst Intendant under 3 years service	Asst Doctor under 3 years service

Midshipmen's, Cadets' and Chief Petty Officers' Insignia

Midshipmen, cadets and chief petty officers wore the same cap badge: the crown above the oval cockade with foul anchor superimposed, surrounded by a wreath of four oak leaves, the whole embroidered in gold.

Midshipmen and cadets wore a $\frac{9}{32}$ in (7 mm) wide stripe of gold lace on the cuffs, with the curl for 'A' Class and without the curl for ordinary midshipmen and cadets.

The chief petty officers used a different type of gold lace stripe $\frac{13}{32}$ in (10 mm) in width, $3\frac{1}{2}$ in (90 mm) in length; the stripes were placed at $\frac{7}{32}$ in (5 mm) from each other, the lowest at $2\frac{3}{4}$ in (70 mm) from the sleeve's edge in the case of C.P.O. 1st Grade, at $3\frac{5}{16}$ in (85 mm) for C.P.O. 2nd Grade and at $3\frac{15}{16}$ in (100 mm) for the 3rd Grade. They wore golden metal corps badges on the collar of the jacket.

Plate 17. Petty Officers' and Seamen's Insignia

The cap badge for petty officers was made of brass, in two pieces: the crown and anchor, and the wreath, and was placed on the peaked cap above a round silk cockade.

The chevrons were $\frac{9}{16}$ in (14 mm) wide and $3\frac{1}{2}$ in (90 mm) long on the side and were sewn at $\frac{9}{32}$ in (7 mm) from each other. Yellow chevrons were used on blue uniform and blue chevrons on white uniform.

There were petty officers of 1st and 2nd Class with three and two chevrons respectively; a single chevron insignia existed as well and was worn by the Reservist Leader of the fire brigade at naval bases.

Cap tallies with the name of ships were used from 1909 until about 1932 and were then replaced by the 'KGL. MARINE', i.e. 'Royal Navy' type for all. The tally was $1\frac{1}{8}$ in (28 mm) wide and the letters were $\frac{13}{32}$ in (12 mm) high; on its right side there was a red-white-red Dannebrøg cockade and on the left the tally was knotted into a bow.

Trade Badges

Conscripted able-bodied seamen wore a red crown above the anchor on both upper sleeves, while qualified tradesmen wore yellow badges woven on black silk, as illustrated.

Germany

The 'Kriegsmarine' of the Third Reich traced its origins to the small fleet of Prussia but most of these ships were ceded to Sweden in 1815. A new programme of naval development started in 1835 but, after the Danish–German War of 1848–50, most ships were sold.

In 1853 Prussia acquired what is now the port of Wilhelmshaven from the State of Oldenburg, and Kiel in 1865 after another war against Denmark.

The Prime Minister Otto von Bismarck's ambition was to unite all German States into one realm with a powerful army and navy and the first obvious step to achieve the latter was to secure the best harbours available.

By the time of the Franco–Prussian War, the North German Federation had thirty-seven warships, which included three armoured frigates, but the real rise of the fleet coincided with the rule of Emperor Wilhelm II; his navy became one of the strongest in the world and the construction of the Kiel Canal, between the Baltic and the North Sea, became a factor of great strategic importance.

Squadrons went to Africa and China; in 1897 the naval personnel numbered twenty-three thousand and sixty-five thousand by the outbreak of World War 1.

The Treaty of Versailles reduced drastically the strength of the German Navy and, by 1935, a naval treaty between Britain and Germany limited the latter's navy to 35 per cent of the strength of the Royal Navy.

This treaty was repudiated before the outbreak of World War 2. The uniforms of the 'Kriegsmarine' were derived from those of the 'Reichsmarine', which in turn were developed from the uniforms of the 'Kaiserliche Marine'.

Plate 18. Cap and Rank Insignia

The officers, warrant officers and midshipmen used the same cap badges. The eagle and cockade with wreath were worn on the peaked cap; the former was usually made of gilded brass although embroidered badges were used as well, especially towards the end of the War. The black, white and red national cockade was trimmed with gold wire and the wreath, of twelve oak leaves and four acorns, was embroidered in gold.

A smaller embroidered eagle and the cockade alone were worn on the front of the navy blue side cap by officers, warrant officers and midshipmen, whilst the other ratings had machine embroidered badges, a yellow eagle and a plain black, white and red cockade. Metal badges were worn on the ratings' hat, above the tally.

All officers had the cap's visor covered with blue cloth and bound with black leather on which flag officers displayed gold oak leaves in two rows, senior naval officers (Captain, Commander and Lieutenant-Commander) one row only of oak leaves and junior officers a gold waved rim. In 1963, these embroideries were adopted by the 'Bundeswehr'. Gold piping on the side cap denoted officer's rank.

Rank was shown by means of cuff stripes and shoulder cords in the usual naval fashion; however, as it was generally difficult for army personnel to identify naval ranks, naval officers who worked with the army often wore shoulder straps on the blue jacket as well.

The German officers had their stripes higher on the sleeves than did British or American officers. Flag officers wore a large gold lace stripe, combined with from one to four medium stripes above it, and shoulder cords formed by two gold and one silver plaited stripes of braid, with silver 4-pointed stars, or pips, to identify each individual rank.

As usual with German military tradition, the lowest rank in each specific class did not wear the pip, the Great Admiral had crossed batons on the shoulder cords instead of pips and, like the General Admiral, wore one broad and four medium stripes on the cuffs. The rank of Commodore was seldom used: he wore a single large gold stripe on the cuffs and shoulder cords, as for a Captain.

The cloth backing to the shoulder cords of all officers of the active list, regardless of branch, matched in colour the uniform on which they had to be worn.

Plate 19. Officers' Rank Insignia

Executive officers or officers of the Line wore a 5-pointed star above the cuff stripes and no device on the shoulder cords, while those of the other branches were identified by embroidered badges on the cuffs, in place of the star and by metal badges on the shoulder cords. The flag officers' badges were made of silver and those of the other officers of gilded brass, to match the metal of the pips. The following were the branches and corresponding badges:

Branch	**Badge**
Line	Star
Engineering	Cogwheel
Medical	Aesculapius staff
Ordnance	Crossed cannons
Defensive Ordnance	Mine
Coast Artillery	Winged grenade

Branch	Badge
Communications	Lightning
Technical Communications	Cogwheel above lightning
Torpedo Technician	Torpedo above cogwheel
Administration	Winged caduceus
Intendance	As above on gold bar
Legal	Sword above gold bar

The last two branches were organised in 1944 from officers formerly belonging to the service of Administrative Officials. Their badges had a gold bar below, $\frac{19}{32}$ in × $\frac{7}{32}$ in (15 mm × 5 mm) in size, made of lace. Reserve officers wore two small gold oak leaves below the branch badge.

The shoulder cords were basically the same as those of the army; those for senior and junior officers were made of silver braid, plaited for the former and straight for the latter, with buttons, pips and badges of gilded brass.

Plate 20. Breast Insignia

All ranks of the German Navy wore the national insignia, the eagle, on the right breast of the uniform and, therefore, of course, there were innumerable variations in relation to style and manufacture. Basically, the officers wore gold embroidered eagles on blue uniforms and gilded badges with a pin at the back on white uniforms; the ratings' badges were silk woven or machine embroidered in yellow cotton, on a navy blue background.

These badges were considerably larger than those worn on the cap.

Chaplains' Badges

The chaplains were classed as Administrative Officials with officers' status but without a definite rank and therefore without conventional rank insignia.

They wore a silver cap badge, with the Roman Cross in between the eagle and the cockade, silver breast insignia and silver buttons. Their collar patches were embroidered in silver and depicted the cross above two oak leaves and acorns on a violet background.

Midshipmen's and Chief Petty Officers' Rate Insignia

The midshipmen wore silver shoulder cords which could be described as 'half' shoulder cords, because they were made with only one double strand of silver braid turned back around the button hole. The Senior Midshipman wore two silver pips, the ordinary Midshipman none and branch badges of officer's type were added between the pips or on the plain cords by the non-executive midshipmen. The gold star, or branch badges were shown on the cuffs as illustrated.

Ratings graduated in their own particular department and initially wore the round badges illustrated on Plate 22; on achieving Petty Officers' rate they changed to the badges on Plate 21, with additional anchor, and eventually graduated to wearing shoulder straps, with small departmental badges made of brass.

The shoulder straps were made of blue cloth, edged by gold lace of special naval pattern and carried silver pips according to rate and the departmental badge.

The various departmental rates developed independently one from another, each with different titles, and equivalent rates were not necessarily represented by the same number of pips, nor were the pips placed in the same position.

Plate 21. Petty Officers' Badges

The petty officers wore, on the left upper sleeve, the departmental badge combined with an anchor, except for those of the Line who wore the anchor alone and the Boatswain who had crossed anchors.

The senior petty officers had a small chevron below the badge and the Candidate Officer had two chevrons, one smaller than the other.

These badges were embroidered in yellow silk on a dark blue background for use on blue uniforms, or in medium blue silk or wool on white for white uniforms. Brass badges were worn on the 'Uberzieher', i.e. the short overcoat, and on the parade jacket, with two rows of buttons at the front and the buttons on the cuff tabs.

Chief petty officers wore officers' type uniform, while the petty officers wore sailors' uniforms, naval hat with tally, jumper and, in cold weather, the short overcoat mentioned above.

On 1 December 1939 medium blue collar patches were adopted for wearing on the overcoat, with one gold stripe for petty officers and two for senior petty officers.

The cap tally usually displayed the type and name of the ship or organisation to which a sailor was attached, but all were replaced by the 'KRIEGSMARINE' (Navy of War) tally illustrated. In 1940 the side cap was introduced as a more practical type of head-dress, in variations and with different badges according to rate.

Plate 22. Departmental Badges

The departmental badges, in yellow on dark blue or blue on white, according to type of uniform, were worn on the left upper sleeve above eventual chevrons.

All except two accord with the badges illustrated in the previous plates; the device of the Line department for seamen was the star, as for the officers' branch, and the badge of the admirals' staff had no counterpart among those of higher ratings.

Seamen's Rate Badges

The chevrons of the seamen identified rate and long service at the same time. Those of the two upper ranks were made of plaited gold braid and the others of gold lace of naval pattern, and were adopted in 1936, although their designations were subsequently modified in 1938 and in 1940.

A smaller silver lace chevron or stripe below these ratings' badges denoted that the wearer was respectively awaiting promotion to petty officer's rate or in training for promotion.

Plate 23. War Awards and Clasps

Eight badges were introduced during World War 2 as a reward for individuals or crews who had achieved special merits in action; all were worn on the left breast.

The Submarines' War Badge was adopted in January 1918 and re-instituted in October 1939 for crews who had been engaged in at least two operational sorties, or one particularly successful sorty.

The Destroyers' War Badge was instituted in June 1940 and was also awarded to crews of motor torpedo boats until May 1941, when the E-Boats received their own award; the badge of the latter had initially a silver central device and, later, from January 1943 onward, the central part was made of grey metal and the boat protruded well out of the oak wreath frame, as illustrated.

Personnel of minesweepers, anti-submarine and escort vessels were granted a badge, in August 1940, that was awarded for participation in three operational sorties, or one that was particularly successful.

The auxiliary cruisers were, in fact, armed merchant ships and their crews obtained badges in April 1941; a special badge with diamonds was awarded for exceptional merit.

The High Seas Fleet War Badge was instituted in April 1941 to reward crews of battleships and cruisers for 13 weeks of active service at sea, or single successful actions. A higher award with diamonds existed as well.

Individuals usually could obtain a badge for having been wounded in action or if their ship was sunk in action.

The Coast Artillery War Badge was instituted in June 1941 and was awarded on the basis of points gained for spotting, detecting and shooting down enemy aircraft, eight being the requisite number.

All the badges above were oval in shape and all followed a basic pattern: they carried the German Eagle on top, a central device which identified the award and an oval frame of gold oak leaves and acorns. The Blockade Runners' Badge was different because it was round in shape and was made of black metal, except for the eagle and the chain around the badge, which were silver. It was instituted in April 1941 for crews of German merchant vessels who succeeded in bringing their ships back home or scuttled them to avoid enemy capture, who managed to get back home after their ship was sunk or who were wounded as a result of enemy action.

As German submariners performed great deeds of valour, year after year, throughout the war, Grand Admiral Doenitz instituted a Submarine War Badge with diamonds which was awarded to submarines' commanders for exceptional merit and, in May 1944, the Submarine Combat Clasp started to be issued to crews. The first clasp was made of bronze and a second one, of silver, was instituted in the following November and later a gilt clasp as well, but the latter probably was never awarded.

The Naval Combat Clasp was created in November 1944, in one single bronze version, as an additional reward for those who already possessed a naval war badge. All naval personnel were eligible except submariners, who had their own clasps. It was awarded to individuals who fulfilled a further five times the conditions required for obtaining a war badge and was worn above the ribbon bars.

The Small Fighting Means ('Kleinkampfmittel') was a new naval branch created in the autumn of 1943 and, as its title suggests, it consisted of frogmen, manned torpedoes and midget submarines, etc. deployed in unconventional naval warfare.

A sawfish was the emblem of this new branch and, therefore, when on 30 November 1944 war badges were instituted, the sawfish became their main device. The badge of the first four classes was worn on the right upper sleeve and consisted of the emblem embroidered in gold or yellow on a blue circular patch, as illustrated. The 7th Class badge was given after 2 months' service in the branch, the 6th Class was awarded for participation in one combat action, the 5th in two and so on. A bronze clasp was awarded for five actions, silver clasp for seven actions and gilt clasp, the 1st Class, for ten or more combat actions. The clasps were worn above ribbon bars, or above the left breast pocket.

Cadets' Badges

The cadets wore sailors' uniform and were distinguished from their shipmates by the badges they had on the left sleeve, in place of the departmental insignia.

The badge depicted the emblem of the officers' branch for which the cadet was training, surrounded by an oval frame, the whole in gold on blue or blue on a white background.

The badge of Defensive Ordnance was the last to be adopted, possibly in 1940.

Plates 24, 25. Trade Badges

The trade badge was worn on the left sleeve, below rate insignia. Some incorporated small chevrons, which in some cases denoted seniority of specialisation, grade or class of specialisation or attendance at specific courses.

Two small oak leaves and one acorn below the emblem identified a specialist of the Reserve.

In August 1940 a new set of trade badges was adopted and the previous ones were abolished; the following were the new badges:

Grenade with one, two or three chevrons below—for 3rd, 2nd and 1st Gun Leader, respectively.

Winged grenade—for A.A. Gunner and Observer; with one or two chevrons below for 2nd and 1st Gun Leader, respectively.

Rangefinder—for Range Taker; with one chevron below for holder of A.A. certificate and with two chevrons for Range Taker training for petty officers' rate.

Torpedo with one or two chevrons below—for 3rd and 2nd Torpedo Specialist, respectively.

Mine with one chevron below—for Mines Specialist.

Diver's helmet with one, two or three chevrons below—for Ship Diver, Torpedo Diver and Submarine Diver, respectively.

Arrow pointing down with one and two chevrons below—for Underwater Detector Specialists with Seamen's and Petty Officers' Course, respectively.

Arrow pointing up and with one chevron below—Unqualified and Qualified A.A. Detector Listener; with two chevrons below for A.A. Searchlights Specialist Leader.

Wheel with electric sparks and with one or two chevrons below—for Coastal Electrician and Electrotechnician of 3rd and 2nd course, respectively.

3-bladed propeller with one and two chevrons below—for Motor Engineer of 3rd and 2nd Course, respectively.

Grenade ball with three flames, and with two chevrons below—for Coast Artillery Gun Leader, apprentice and specialist, respectively.

Grenade ball with three flames and wings—for A.A. Coast Artillery Gun Leader.

Circle with two converging arrows, and with chevron below—for Armourer Specialist in general and of Artillery, Coastal and A.A. Gunnery.

Two chevrons, the uppermost with a curl—for Drummers and Pipers. Only four of these new badges have been illustrated in the last row of trade badges because they differed from the previous ones; all the others, or at least the main emblems, were the same as those of the old badges.

Bandmasters

Bandmaster and music directors wore officers' uniforms but with special rank insignia, stripes with curl and lyre in the curl on the cuffs and different shoulder cords, which incorporated strands of blue braid, as illustrated.

In 1940 the stripes with curl were abolished and bandmasters were allowed to use the straight gold stripes below the branch badge like all the other naval officers.

The following were their ranks and the corresponding ranks for officers of the Line:

Bandmasters	**Line**
Musikmeister	Leutnant z.S.
Obermusikmeister	Oberleutnant z.S.
Stabsmusikmeister	Kapitänleutnant
Musikinspizient	Korvettenkapitän
Obermusikinspizient	Fregattenkapitän

Plate 26. Badges for Field Grey Uniforms

Naval detachments that served on land, for instance on coastal defence, wore field grey uniforms of army pattern; later in the war the navy raised many battalions and larger formations specifically for land warfare and their personnel used army uniforms as well.

The admirals initially did not wear field grey uniforms and only a few used it later, therefore some items of their dress, for instance the colour of their collar patches, greatcoats' lapels and trousers' stripes are still in controversy; probably it was ultramarine, cornflower or middle blue.

The officers wore on the peaked cap gold naval badges, the wreath embroidered on dark bluish-green felt, gold or silver chin strap cords for admirals and other officers, respectively, and plain black leather visors. The side, or field, cap carried the same badges as the one made of blue cloth, but with badges embroidered on a dark bluish green background. Similarly, all breast eagles were embroidered or woven on dark bluish-green cloth.

The same colour was used as a backing to the silver double bars worn by the officers on the collar, officers' shoulder cords and ratings' shoulder straps.

The admirals' shoulder cords, made of two gold and one silver strand of braid as usual, were placed on a medium blue cloth background but, apart from the background, the cords, rank insignia and button were the same as those used on the blue uniform.

The ratings' insignia were different, as illustrated, because the 'field grey' navy had more rates than the 'blue' navy. During the late stages of the War field grey shoulder straps were issued to the ratings, as the quality of uniforms progressively deteriorated.

The badges illustrated are typical of the 'field grey' navy, although normal branch badges were used as well, for instance doctors wore the Aesculapius staff, etc. Other devices were often worn in combination with branch badges or on their own: the initials 'N' for 'Nordsee', 'O' for 'Ostsee' and Roman or Arabic numbers, all made of brass.

Plate 27. Officials' Insignia

The Officials ('Marinebeamten') were individuals, employed in administrative roles at ministries and other offices connected with the navy, who wore naval uniforms and had rank distinctions equivalent to those of the active service.

The major difference between the personnel of the active list and of the 'Marinebeamten' was that the latter wore all insignia and buttons of silver.

Officials with officers' status wore chin strap cords, in gold for flag ranks and silver for the others, on the peaked cap, instead of embroideries on the visor, which was made of black leather. They had silver lace stripes on the cuffs below the Administrative Officials' badge, the German Eagle, combined with the branch devices of specific administration.

All these oval-shaped badges have been illustrated; usually three devices identified an official with a university degree while two or one branch devices were worn by those with lesser qualifications. Eight devices were in existence in 1939 and two more were added to the active list: Intendance and Legal, with personnel drawn from the Administrative Officials.

Officials' shoulder cords and pips were the same as those of the navy but were placed on underlay of different colours, as in the following list:

Branch	Colour
Supreme Command of the Navy	Dark blue
Administrative Officials, Pharmacists, Non-technical Teachers of Naval Schools	Cornflower blue
Legal Officials	Crimson
Technicians, Ship's Pilots	Black

Senior ratings wore special cords made of plaited strands of blue and white braid, with the eagle, branch device and one or two pips according to rate, the whole on arm-of-service colour underlay.

Also the officials used field grey uniforms with insignia, in this case on a dark bluish-green background, as already described in the section dealing with naval field grey uniforms.

The designation 'Sonderführer' means 'Special Leader' and referred to specialists with particular qualifications, but without naval training, who served in the navy. Those ranking as officers had small gold foul anchors on the collar and ratings wore the anchor attached to the blue collar patches, below the gold braid.

France

Until the period of the late Consulate there was no uniformity of naval dress; crewmen especially wore what was provided by their officers or were left to their own resources. The first uniforms appeared in 1804 and were, at least for the sailors, rather austere, in complete contrast with those worn a few years later during the period of the Empire. These uniforms were magnificent but had no naval character whatsoever.

The Restoration suppressed all the luxury and the sailors' dress was left once again to the discretion of their commanders until the 1820s, when at least some garments were issued especially to the sailors. The outlook of the 'matelot' began to appear under the reign of Louis Philippe; the sailors were issued with a straw hat ornamented by a ribbon which displayed the name of the ship in gold letters. The collar with three white stripes, the predecessor of the modern one, appeared at that time also.

The woollen tuft on top of the hat was introduced during the period of the Second Empire and was red and white at that time, but it was only in the period of the Third Republic that naval uniforms began to assume the practical features of the modern dress.

The process of modernisation was, however, rather slow; for instance, summer uniforms were officially adopted only in 1929 and special uniforms and utility garments appeared later, in the 1930s.

Plate 28. Flag Officers' Cap and Rank Insignia

The cap badge of the flag officers was embroidered in gold on dark blue cloth and consisted of a wreath of ten laurel leaves with a plain foul anchor for the officers of the corps, an anchor with additional wings and lightnings for executive flag officers.

Special gold embroideries on the cap band distinguished the flag officers from the other officers and, at the same time, identified their rank and corps. Small 5-pointed stars were displayed at the front and the type of embroidery also identified rank, as follows: the Admiral of the Fleet, Admiral and Vice-Admiral of Squadron had an additional stripe of silver braid along the top of the cap band, the Vice-Admiral used the same embroidery as the upper ranks but without the silver braid and the Rear-Admiral had a plainer type of embroidery.

Flag officers of the executive branch ('Officiers de marine') were called admirals while those of the other corps were called generals.

The embroidery of the former depicted oak leaves and acorns while the generals had their own distinctive embroideries, according to corps, full embroideries for the top ranking generals and a plainer pattern for the lower rank, as mentioned above. The embroidery of the medical officers, pharmacists and chemists, for instance, depicted laurel leaves and snakes, commissaries had oak and vine leaves, engineers of naval artillery had olive leaves and crossed cannons above anchors and engineers of hydrography had plain olive leaves.

Gold chin strap cords were worn by admirals and generals on the peaked cap. They also used another cap for duties on board ship: it had a plain cap band, leather chin strap and an oval-shaped badge at the front which displayed the rank stars.

Rank insignia in the form of stars were worn on the cuffs and on the shoulder straps; the latter were edged with a gold stripe and carried a foul anchor and the stars were on the outer ends.

Plain rectangular shoulder tabs embroidered in gold were worn on the blue jacket; four patterns existed, according to class of rank.

The rank of Admiral of the Fleet was created for Admiral Darlan on 6 June 1939 and remained in existence until his death in 1942. He wore two stars above three on the embroidered cap band while, on the cuffs and shoulder straps, one star was always placed above the other four, as illustrated.

The officers of the corps could usually graduate to two flag ranks, although pharmacists, for example, could attain only one. Their rank titles were preceded by the corps' name, for instance:

'Médecin Général de 1ère Classe'	Medical—Vice-Admiral
'Commissaire Général de 1ère Classe'	Commissariat—Vice-Admiral
'Pharmacien Général de 2ème Classe'	Pharmacy—Rear-Admiral

The officers of the Fleet Equipage (Officiers des Équipages de la Flotte') did not reach flag rank as their top rank was 'Officier en Chef des Équipages de la Flotte' which corresponded to the executive rank of 'Capitaine de Frégate'. Musicians graduated up to the rank of 'Chef de Musique Principal', i.e. 'Capitaine de Corvette'.

Plate 29. Officers' Cap and Rank Insignia

The cap badge of the officers below flag rank had only eight leaves in the wreath and the foul anchor in its centre. They displayed their rank in the form of lace stripes on the cap band and on the cuffs, and on the shoulder straps.

The executive officers had their stripes attached to the sleeve, or dark blue shoulder straps, while the officers of corps had the stripes on coloured backing which protruded $3\frac{18}{8}$ in (100 mm) above and below the stripes and wore coloured shoulder straps without the anchor.

The following coloured velvet backings were used:

Corps	Colour
Directors of Music	Blue-grey
Mechanical Officers	Violet
Interpreters and Naval Cypher Officers	Ultramarine
Naval Engineers of various specialities	Black
Commissariat	Otter brown
Medical	Crimson
Chemists and Pharmacists	Light green
Hydrographical Professors	Light violet
Recruiting and Administrative Staff	Ash grey

The officers of the Fleet Equipage were specialists who had been commissioned from the ranks and were distinguished by a rectangular patch with button on the cuffs and shoulder straps.

Rank titles varied as shown in the following scheme:

Executive Branch	Fleet Équipage	Corps
Capitaine de Vaisseau	—	en Chef de 1ère Classe
Capitaine de Frégate	en Chef	en Chef
Capitaine de Corvette	Principal	Principal
Lieutenant de Vaisseau	de 1ère Classe	de 1ère Classe
Enseigne de Vaisseau de 1ère Classe	de 2ème Classe	de 2ème Classe
Enseigne de Vaisseau de 2ème Classe	—	de 3ème Classe

The designation of the officers' corps was placed before the rank titles, as for example 'Médecin de 1ère classe' in the case of a Doctor. Officers of the Fleet Equipage had 'Officier' in front of their rank title.

Plate 30. Cap and Rate Insignia

The insignia of midshipmen, petty officers, quartermasters, etc. have been illustrated in this plate.

A foul anchor surrounded by a wreath of two laurel leaves only was the cap badge of the Midshipman and of the ratings who were entitled to wear the peaked cap. The gold badge was used by personnel of the Fleet Equipage, musicians, firemen, signalmen and harbour personnel, while the red badge was used by musicians, firemen, signalmen and harbour personnel only.

The Midshipman, the senior petty officers and others, while wearing special uniform, wore gold cap badges; the Midshipman, Chief and 1st Petty Officer and the Petty Officer had also a gold stripe of lace around the cap band.

All wore rate insignia on the cuffs and, down to 2nd Petty Officer, on the shoulder straps as well; lower ratings had stripes on the cuffs only.

The Midshipman's stripe was gold and blue and, like the stripes of the Chief and 1st Petty Officer, was worn straight, horizontally. The Petty Officer and 2nd Petty Officer used lace of special pattern, in the form of chevrons on the shoulder straps and oblique stripes on cuffs. The large stripe was $\frac{7}{8}$ in (22 mm) in width, the narrow one $\frac{15}{32}$ in (12 mm) and the narrow stripes were placed at a distance of $\frac{5}{64}$ in (2 mm) from each other, with the lower end at $3\frac{1}{2}$ in (90 mm) from the bottom edge of the sleeve, the higher end at $7\frac{1}{16}$ in (180 mm).

The Quartermaster ('Quartier-Maître de Maistrance') qualified at the 'École de Maistrance' and wore a gold and blue stripe on the cuffs. The junior quartermasters had three or two red stripes according to class and the Qualified Seaman a single large one.

The junior ratings wore a special badge on the left breast of the summer vest; it depicted a blue anchor surrounded by a blue rectangular frame and with blue stripes at the bottom which identified rate class.

Plate 31. Cap, Rate and Speciality (on collar) Insignia

Some specialists were entitled to different insignia: tailors wore stripes of gold and red lace, yeomen wore gold stripes on the upper sleeves and buglers were identified by an additional stripe sewn along the edge of the sleeves, as illustrated.

The gold foul anchor was worn by junior ratings on the blue hat, above the tally, but not on the white hat of the summer uniform. A larger anchor $2\frac{9}{16}$ in (65 mm) in width, cut out from red cloth, was worn on the left side of the blue cap used by naval mechanics and drivers. The same badge was also worn on both sides of the collar of coats and overcoats by junior ratings of the Fleet Equipage.

All the other badges were worn in pairs on the collar of jackets and tunics, in gold or red according to the colour of the cap badge and of the rate insignia. Musicians had the lyre on the shoulder straps as well. The personnel of the Naval Police wore army type uniforms with all their insignia and buttons of silver. They were distinguished by the wearing of silver anchors on the kepi and on the collar of the tunic.

Speciality and Other Badges

Naval aviators wore speciality badges made of metal on the right breast. All consisted of a silver anchor superimposed on to a rope, gold wings and a 5-pointed star for aircraft personnel or wings and a steering wheel for airship or balloon personnel.

The specialities of the aircraft crew included mechanics, telegraphists, machine-gunners, bombardiers and observers.

Physical Training Instructors of the navy wore the same badge as the instructors of the army, in gold or silver according to rank. The badge was pinned on the left side of the breast.

After 1940, France continued to fight together with the Allies and the new French Navy was designated 'Forces Navales Françaises Libres' and adopted the Cross of Lorraine as their emblem.

The officers wore, on the breast, an enamelled, diamond-shaped badge; the sailors had a plainer badge, embroidered in blue, white and red, with gold edges.

A number of enamelled badges were used by personnel of some vessels, of which one has been illustrated: it was the badge of the torpedo boat *Combattante* and depicts the French cockerel and the Cross of Lorraine.

Plate 32. Speciality Insignia (on sleeves)

The junior ratings of the Fleet Equipage wore crossed anchors, cut out from red cloth, on the right sleeve, while speciality insignia were worn on the left sleeve. Holders of a superior certificate had a gold embroidered 5-pointed star, with the top point downwards, on both sleeves above the rate stripes.

The submarines had crossed torpedoes and lightnings, $2\frac{3}{4}$ in (70 mm) wide, embroidered in gold or red thread. The fusiliers were marines embarked on ships and wore the flaming grenade in gold, silver or red, according to rate and qualification.

The radio-telegraphist on coastal duty held a temporary brevet of General Service and wore a red badge, while those on permanent duty of General Service had the gold badge.

The crossed cannons of the Gun Aimer and his proficiency star were made of red cloth, in contrast to the other badges which were embroidered. The proficiency stars were placed at $1\frac{3}{16}$ in (30 mm) above the speciality badge.

The cap tallies used before the war displayed the name of the ship or of a corps to which an individual could be assigned, later the tallies of the Free French Navy carried the initials 'F.N.F.L.' only.

Italy

The Italian Royal Navy was derived from the Sardinian Navy, which traced its origins to a single galley that Amedeus V, County of Savoy, had built in 1287 for sailing on the Lake of Geneva. By 1316 a fleet of four galleys patrolled the lake and, after 1388, when Nice was taken over by the County of Savoy, an access was gained to the Mediterranean, and more galleys were built there as a defence against pirates.

The first major battle in which Savoy's vessels participated was fought at Lepanto in October 1571, against the Turks. At that time a ship's crew was composed of the officers of the upper stern, the leading seamen, embarked soldiers and the crew 'at the oars'.

By the beginning of the eighteenth century, the fleet was divided into two squadrons, galleys and sailships and a battalion of permanent marines was assigned to the former, contrary to the previous rule of embarking any unit on foot when necessary. However, two regiments called 'La Marina' were formed previously but fought on land with the French Army. A third one was raised in 1714 and, a few years later, absorbed the battalion of marines mentioned above; one battalion was deployed on land duties and the other on ships.

Eventually, in 1798, the regiment became part of the French Army, it was disbanded in 1800 and re-formed in 1814 as an infantry regiment. Meanwhile, another battalion of marines was formed in Sardinia, but it was only after the Restoration and the acquisition of Genoa and the region of Liguria that the growth of the navy became in earnest.

The period of Victor Emmanuel II's rule (1849–78) was the most eventful in respect of naval expansion as, due to its process of unification, Italy became a seafaring nation, because of its geographical position in the centre of the Mediterranean sea.

The Royal Decree of 17 November 1860 established the Italian Royal Navy, born by the amalgamation of the Sardinian, Borbonic and Sicilian, Tuscan and Papal navies. The whole service was restructured and, through subsequent reorganisations, it became the modern Italian Royal Navy of the twentieth century.

Plate 33. Head-dress Insignia

Officers, chiefs and senior petty officers wore the peaked cap with gold embroidered naval badge: the corps' badge on an oval background called a 'shield', surrounded by six laurel leaves, the whole ensigned by the crown.

There were three types of badges, according to rank:

1. For Great Admiral, with Royal Crown with gold cushion and purple base.
2. For flag officers with the rank of Admiral of Army (Fleet) and Admiral of Squad in Command of Army, with Royal Crown with purple cushion and base.
3. For all other ranks, with Royal Crown with blue cushion and base.

The central badge and the distinction cloth of the shield varied according to corps:

Corps	Badge	Distinction Cloth
Line	Foul anchor	Blue velvet
Naval Engineers	Roman helmet, axe and hammer superimposed on anchor	Crimson velvet
Naval Ordnance	Sword superimposed on anchor	Avana brown felt
Doctors	Red cross superimposed on anchor	White felt
Chemists–Pharmacists	Aesculapius staff	Green felt
Commissariat	Star superimposed on anchor	Purple felt
Port Captaincy	Foul anchor	Grey-green felt

The above were the basic corps but special badges and distinction cloths were used by the following as well:

Chaplains	Gold cross superimposed on anchor	Violet silk
Mechanical Engineers	3-bladed propeller superimposed on anchor	Crimson velvet

The latter were officers serving in the Temporary Role for Machinist Officers, an offspring of the Naval Engineers.

The corps that, for the sake of brevity, has been termed 'Line' included all the executive officers of the General Staff (Stato Maggiore (di Vascello)) and of the Royal Corps of Maritime Crews ('Corpo Reale Equipaggi Marittimi').

The Medical Corps was subdivided into a Medical Role, i.e. doctors, and Pharmacists' Role, composed of chemists and pharmacists.

The personnel of the Naval Ordnance used another corps' badge also which depicted a crossed cannon and torpedo with lightnings at the sides.

All the corps' badges were made of brass.

The officers and chiefs displayed rank insignia on the cap band. Flag officers had a gold embroidered 'greca', the traditional emblem of Italian admirals and generals, surmounted by gold stripes of braid, numbered according to rank.

Senior officers wore one large gold lace stripe with one to three narrower ones above, according to rank, and junior officers had only the narrow stripes around the cap band. Two or more stripes were woven in one piece with black (Line) or coloured intervals on the outer edgings, according to corps.

The chiefs had one stripe only on the cap, regardless of class; their stripe was made of gold lace and blue silk. The other senior petty officers entitled to wear the peaked cap had a plain cap band.

The officers' insignia on the cap corresponded with the rank badges they wore on the cuffs.

Plate 34. Flag Officers' Rank Insignia

The officers of the line had naval rank titles while those of the other corps had army titles. As usual, in an effort to avoid confusion, the officers' rank titles have been left in the original language and the flag officers' titles have been translated literally into English. The Italian admirals were in command of 'armate', 'squadre' and 'divisioni', as the fleet was subdivided in this manner, and, therefore, in this context, these terms are purely nautical.

Shoulder straps were worn, as usual, on white jackets and overcoats, shoulder tabs and cuff stripes on blue jackets. Gold stripes all around the cuffs were displayed on the pre-war dress frock coat only.

The flag officers' shoulder straps were made of gold lace and carried a gold embroidered border, the crown, corps badge and rank insignia in the form of 5-pointed stars; those of the Admiral of Squad in Command of Army had a small crown embroidered in gold wire on blue velvet above the stars and just below the corps badge. All shoulder straps were piped with appropriate distinction cloth, lined at the back with white cloth, and were attached to the jacket by means of a tongue and a gilt button with screw fitting.

The flag officers' shoulder tabs measured $3\frac{3}{16}$ in $\times$ $1\frac{3}{8}$ in (80 mm $\times$ 35 mm) in size; they were made of navy blue felt, lined with white cloth, with coloured piping, as on the shoulder straps, and carried a gold embroidered outer border or frame, the crown and the corps badge. The following badges and distinction cloth were used on shoulder straps and tabs:

Corps	Badge	Distinction Cloth
Line (S.M.)	Foul anchor	Blue felt
Line (C.R.E.M.)	Foul anchor	Black velvet
Naval Engineers	Roman helmet, axe and hammer surrounded by a wreath	Crimson velvet

Corps	Badge	Distinction Cloth
Naval Ordnance	Sword superimposed on anchor	Avana brown felt
Doctors	Aesculapius staff	Light blue felt
Chemists–Pharmacists	Aesculapius staff	Green felt
Commissariat	Gold laurel wreath	Purple felt
Port Captaincy	Foul anchor	Grey-green felt

The generals of the naval ordnance wore the badge alone, without the wreath, on the shoulder tabs.

The type of crown, in relation to the cushion and base, matched the crown of the cap badge, as in the previous plate.

The main rank insignia were worn on the cuffs, at $3\frac{1}{2}$ in (90 mm) from the bottom of the sleeve and consisted of the 'greca' and stripes, 3 in (75 mm) in length, the latter surmounted by a round curl, the whole embroidered in gold. The admirals' badges were embroidered on navy blue cloth, those of the generals of corps were also embroidered on navy blue but their stripes and curls were edged in corps' colour.

The officers and senior petty officers who served on submarines wore a special brass badge on the breast; it depicted a dolphin, surrounded by a wreath and ensigned by the crown.

Plate 35. Officers' Rank Insignia

The shoulder straps of the officers were made of navy blue cloth and were similar in shape and size to those of the flag officers. Senior officers' straps had a gold embroidered border stripe, the crown and rank stars, and those of the junior officers had the crown and stars only. First lieutenants had a small embroidered bar on the outer end of their shoulder straps. No corps' badges were worn on the shoulder straps, but the crown alone, for all.

The shoulder tabs of the senior officers were 3 in × 1 in (75 mm × 25 mm) in size, with coloured piping, gold embroidered border and central rope on dark blue background. Junior officers' tabs consisted of a stripe of gold lace, sewn above a patch of distinction cloth which protruded all around the gold lace.

Gold lace stripes were displayed on the cuffs: the senior officers had a large stripe, $\frac{23}{32}$ in (20 mm) wide, and from one to three narrower ones $\frac{15}{32}$ in (12 mm), the top one with the curl; the junior officers had the narrow stripes only. Stripes and curl were sewn on navy blue cloth or distinction cloth, according to corps.

Until 1936 the specialist officers used rank stripes without the curl. They were usually commissioned from the ranks due to long service and high performance in specialised tasks.

Plate 36. Petty Officers' Rate Insignia and Trade Badges

The rate of Chief ('capo'). in three Classes, corresponded to the army rank of Warrant Officer and therefore the chiefs had officers' type uniform and special stripes on the shoulder straps, together with a speciality badge embroidered in gold.

The next two ratings, the Second Chief and Sergeant, were identified by chevrons, one large and two narrow, one large and one narrow, woven in one piece with blue intervals, with a gold speciality badge on top.

The Junior Chief, Substitute Junior Chief and Seaman 1st Class had red woven chevrons, one large and two narrow in the case of the former, a medium one $\frac{5}{16}$ in (8 mm) for the substitute and a narrow chevron $\frac{7}{32}$ in (5 mm) for the Seaman 1st Class. Red badges were used with red chevrons, or on their own in order to identify the seaman's trade.

The conscripted seaman wore a plain red embroidered anchor on both upper sleeves, others graduated to a red trade badge, to red chevrons and later to petty officers' gold chevrons and gold badges.

The red badges were rather small, the largest on average about $1\frac{3}{8}$ in (35 mm) in width and the gold ones were smaller still. Sailors with a university degree or high school diploma were automatically eligible for the 'L' (Laurea) or 'D' (Diploma) badges, respectively. Buglers did not qualify for petty officers' rate and therefore only the red badge existed.

Plate 37. Trade Badges

Although trade badges were usually embroidered in red cotton, in the case of volunteers with specific trades, as illustrated, gold letters were worn above the usual trade badge. Lower ratings embarked on submarines wore a special badge on the left upper sleeve: it depicted the usual submariners' dolphin in a circle inscribed 'SOMMERGIBILI' $1\frac{25}{32}$ in (45 mm) in diameter, the whole in white metal.

The volunteer second chiefs and conscripted seamen who re-enlisted for the period of 1 year were allowed to wear a $1\frac{9}{16}$ in (40 mm) gold or red stripe, respectively, on both lower sleeves below the volunteer's badge, the Savoy Knot.

Cap Tallies

A vast array of Italian naval cap tallies can still be found, all woven in yellow silk on a black ribbon and a selection have been illustrated.

The first tally is the war-time pattern worn by all ships' personnel, the translation of which reads 'Royal Navy'. Others were worn in the same period, or earlier: *REGIE NAVI* (Royal Ships), *M.A.S.* (Motoscafo Anti-

Sommergibile—Anti-Submarine Motor Boat), *SILURANTI* (Motor Torpedo Boats), *R.CAPITANERIA DI PORTO* (Royal Port Captaincy), *R.GUARDIA DI FINANZA* (Royal Customs Guard), etc. Before the war there were cap tallies with the name of the ships, like for instance *R.N.BIXIO* and *R.N.ANDREA DORIA*, in which case 'R.N.' stands for 'Regia Nave', i.e. 'royal ship'. There were others, like for example *R.CT.NULLO* and *R.CT. FOLGORE*, or *R.SOMM. BALILLA* which identified the type of vessel, 'CT' for 'Cacciatorpediniera' and 'SOMM.' for 'Sommergibile'.

The third tally 'NINO BIXIO' represents the pattern worn during World War 1. Some tallies have chevron-like devices on one or both ends which do not identify rank but are purely ornamental and, at the same time, prevent the tally from unthreading.

Badges of 'SAN MARCO' Marines

The 'San Marco' Regiment derived from the marines of long standing history and other units that fought during World War 1. The former, the 'Reggimento Marina' were formed initially by the 'Monfalcone', 'Grado' and 'Caorle' battalions but, in April 1918, the first battalion was named after Lieutenant-Commander Bafile, and another battalion was formed as well, the 'Golametto'.

The 'Raggruppamento Marina' consisted of naval artillery units deployed on land or on pontoons along the coast.

These two formations were amalgamated in August 1919 into the 'Reggimento San Marco' as, during the late stages of that war, both were deployed on the river Piave and Adriatic coast in the defence of Venice, St Mark's city. The Lion of St Mark badge was introduced at that time, embroidered in gold on red collar patches for officers and petty officers and in yellow cotton on red cuff patches for the other ratings.

Marines were issued with grey-green uniforms of army pattern during World War 1 but retained their badges and naval rank titles, although the officers and senior ratings wore army type rank insignia. The same rules of dress were confirmed after the war: the officers wore grey-green service dress, with peaked cap of naval pattern, shoulder tabs instead of shoulder straps, brown leather Sam Browne belt and black riding boots. Junior ratings and seamen wore the basic naval uniform but made of grey-green cloth and with trousers tucked into puttees; in 1936 their naval hat with tally was replaced by a grey-green beret with a brass Lion of St Mark on a red patch as cap badge. They wore trade badges embroidered in black on a grey-green background on the upper sleeves, on their own or above black chevrons. Seamen without specific specialisation wore the foul anchor.

The officers (and senior petty officers) wore collar patches like the one illustrated at the bottom left of this plate: the Lion of St Mark was embroidered in gold and the star was made of white metal. Initially the patch was sewn at the front of the stand collar and therefore the lions were embroidered horizontally, facing the stars and the opening of the collar. Later, after 1934, when jackets with lapels were adopted, smaller lions were embroidered on the top of the patch, as illustrated. The bottom of the collar patch fitted the bottom of the collar, thus patches with pointed bottom ends were made for pointed collars, as for instance the collar of the British battledress. The cuff patches' device was initially embroidered in yellow wool, later in cotton, or rayon. Junior chiefs had an additional gold stripe sewn at the bottom of their cuff patches.

A special embroidered or metal badge was worn on the left upper sleeve by all personnel of the Swimmers–Parachutists Battalion ('Battaglione Nuotatori Paracadutisti'—N.P.Bn) of the Royal Navy and was used later by the navy of the Social Republic, until it was replaced by another badge.

The Armistice of 8 September 1943 led to the formation of two Italian navies, one in the south which carried on the traditions of the old Royal Navy and another one in the north, as part of the armed forces of the Italian Social Republic.

The badges of the former did not change. The Combat Group 'Folgore' was formed on 24 September 1944 as part of the new Italian armed forces and subsequently took part in the Italian Campaign on the Allies' side. It was constituted by a regiment of parachutists, the 'San Marco' regiment of marines and an artillery regiment.

All the personnel of combat groups wore a similar formation sign, the green-white-red colours with the combat group's emblem in the centre; in the case of the 'Folgore' a lightning' as 'folgore' means 'lightning' in Italian.

All personnel wore British battledress, the marines with dark blue beret with naval cap badge for officers and senior petty officers, and a small brass anchor for other ratings and seamen. They had collar or cuff patches according to rank, as before, until 1945, when cuff patches were adopted for officers as well, instead of collar patches.

The regiment was divided into three battalions, named 'Bafile', 'Grado', and 'Caorle' and a shoulder title of the former exists, embroidered in gold wire; it is not known if the other battalions had shoulder titles as well.

Plate 38. Naval Badges and Insignia of the Italian Social Republic

Northern Italy became a republic after the Armistice, thus crowns and royal emblems were deleted accordingly. In the case of the navy, the crown was cut off from badges, shoulder straps and tabs; later new ones were made with the

Republican Eagle in place of the crown on cap badges and the anchor alone embroidered in the centre of shoulder straps and tabs. Three cap badges have been illustrated, one with the crown cut off, the regulations badge with eagle on the left and a smaller one, possibly for the beret, with incorrect leaves in the wreath.

The national emblem, the white star, was replaced on the collar by the 'gladio', a Roman sword superimposed on a round wreath, and eventually new dress regulations were published, which prescribed chin strap cords for officers and some other Germanic features. However, the personnel as a whole kept on wearing their old uniforms with the new badges which, in any case, except for the lack of royal emblems and the new Republican Eagle, were the same as before.

On 27 May 1944 a set of nine badges was introduced to reward long and distinguished service in war-time: bronze badges (1st Degree) were awarded for 18 months of embarkation, or 1,000 hours of navigation at sea including participation in at least one war engagement. Silver badges (2nd Degree) required 30 months of embarkation or 3,000 hours of navigation and three war engagements, and gold badges (3rd Degree) were given for 48 months of embarkation or 5,000 hours at sea and six war engagements. A set of silver badges only has been illustrated.

As, by then, the naval contingent had become ineffectual, new units of marines were created for fighting on land and their personnel wore grey-green uniforms.

A number of badges, for wearing on the breast or on the left upper sleeve were introduced during this period and have been illustrated in this and the following plate.

Plate 39. Naval Badges and Insignia of the Italian Social Republic

The 3rd Division of Marine Infantry 'San Marco' was formed in March 1944 from units of an Italian grenadiers division in training at Grafenwöhr, Germany. The latter was originally raised in December 1943 from a mixed personnel, mainly Italian sailors picked up in the Aegean and Black Shirts that were in Greece at the time of the Armistice. Others later joined up, mainly ex-marines and sailors.

Meanwhile another unit, which existed before the Armistice, the Xth Flotilla M.A.S., was strengthened in Italy and eventually became a division. The initials 'M.A.S.' stand for 'Motoscafo Anti-Sommergibile', i.e. Anti-Submarine Motor Boat.

The men of both units wore similar uniforms: a grey-green beret with brass anchor at the front, a grey-green jacket originally used by parachutists, virtually a 'sahariana' without collar and lapels, and long, baggy trousers tucked into the boots. Officers and petty officers usually wore riding breeches with boots or puttees. However, the personnel of many units were issued with normal infantry uniforms because of lack of supplies.

All wore naval cap badges and marines' type of collar patches, of different colours, as illustrated. A new Lion of St Mark was adopted during the period of the Social Republic: the badge was made of brass and had a tablet at the base with the motto *iterum rudit leo*, i.e. 'The Lion Still Roars', but, contrary to the previous badge, the lion held a closed book, perhaps an omen of the impending disaster.

All ranks who had completed a period of training in Germany were entitled to wear a special badge on the right breast, on the pocket or above it. Artillery personnel of the 'San Marco' Division had the anchor above crossed cannons on the upper sleeves.

Personnel of the reconnaissance unit of the 'San Marco' wore a special white metal cap badge which depicted a flaming grenade above crossed Roman swords, and special black collar patches with a white skull in place of the Lion of St Mark.

Exactly the same cap badge, the foul anchor in brass, was worn during this period by the marines of the King in the South and by those of Mussolini in the North.

The United States of America

The importance of sea power became apparent to the American public during the Civil War when both the Northern and Southern forces attempted to blockade each other's main ports and coastline. The first major engagement between ironclad ships took place during that conflict.

More experience was gained during the war against Spain which was followed by a period of territorial expansion in which the U.S. Navy played a major role. The opening of the Panama Canal led to a great strategic improvement as the Atlantic and Pacific fleets could communicate and support each other directly through the canal.

An American battle squadron operated with the British Grand Fleet during World War I and innumerable destroyers and submarine chasers of the U.S. Navy gave valid aid to the Allies' cause.

The insignia of the U.S. Navy and of the U.S. Coast Guard have been grouped together as these two organisations wore the same uniforms and the same type of badges. During peace-time, the Coast Guard comes under the Secretary of the Treasury while, in war-time, since 1799, it has been under the direction of the Secretary of the Navy.

Plate 40. Cap Head-dress Insignia

As a general rule, the naval peaked cap matched in colour the rest of the uniform, except for the white cover, which could be worn with the white or with the blue uniform. The cap band was black, to match the background of the cap badge, the visor was made of black leather, covered with blue cloth in the case of senior officers entitled to gold leaves, the chin strap of the officers and warrant officers was made of gold braid while the chief petty officers, officers' cooks and stewards had plain leather chin straps.

There were two types of gold embroideries for the peaked cap's visor: with a double row of gold oak leaves and acorns for flag officers and a single row for the ranks of Captain and Commander; after 1 January 1944, the visor's embroideries were used only on formal occasions, otherwise the plain visor was worn by all. At the same time, a black braid chin strap was introduced for everyday use and the gold one was relegated to formal wear, although, in fact, the black chin strap never turned out to be very popular. Later, the use of the visor's embroideries and gold chin strap became optional.

All naval officers, down to Chief Warrant Officer, wore the same cap badge, which could be found in metal or embroidered versions; initially, until May

1941, the eagle faced to its left, later to its right, towards the wearer's sword arm, the correct heraldic position of honour.

The Warrant Officer's cap badge depicted two crossed foul anchors, the Midshipman wore one gold anchor and the petty officers had the initials 'U.S.N.' in silver superimposed upon the anchor. Officers' cooks and stewards had the initials alone, in brass.

The U.S. Coast Guard had different cap badges, with the United States Shield in prominence, superimposed on the anchors of the warrant officers and petty officers and in the centre of the cap badge worn by Shore Establishment personnel. U.S.C.G. cadets wore the foul anchor in gold ensigned by a silver star and the officers' stewards the initials alone. Most surfmen eventually adopted the cap device of the Shore Establishment but the former badge, illustrated, still remained in use.

The U.S.C.G. officers wore a large American Eagle, with the shield on its chest clutching a horizontal foul anchor.

The nurse's peaked cap was adopted in 1942 for wearing with street uniform: it displayed a left collar badge at the front, above the cap band. The nurse's white cap had a $1\frac{1}{2}$ in (38 mm) black velvet band across the front on which gold lace rank stripes were displayed. The Superintendent of the Navy Nurse Corps, Sue Dauser, became Captain in March 1943 and, together with the administrative commanders, did not wear the white uniform cap but displayed rank by cuff stripes and shoulder straps, in accordance with navy regulations.

Bandsmen wore a special badge on the peaked cap of the dress uniform, which has not been illustrated; it depicted a gold silk or rayon embroidered lyre superimposed upon an anchor. The cap had a red and gold cap band.

The garrison cap could be used by commissioned officers, warrant officers and by chief petty officers and matched the colour of the rest of the uniform; therefore there were blue, white, light khaki, green (winter khaki) and grey garrison caps, with miniature rank insignia on the right side and small cap device on the left for officers, corps devices on both sides for warrant officers and small cap device on the left side only for the Chief Petty officer.

Naval aviators and observers wore miniature aviation wings on the left side of the garrison cap until the spring of 1943 and later changed to the ordinary small naval badges.

Plate 41. Officers' Rank and Corps Insignia

The officers' rank and corps' insignia were usually combined, on the cuffs of the sleeves, shoulder straps and on the khaki shirt's collar.

Cuff stripes are the conventional naval officers' rank distinction and were shown in gold on dress and blue service coats, in black on overcoats and green winter working aviation coats, with the black Line star in the latter case; corps devices were not worn on the overcoat.

The overcoat carried cuff stripes and shoulder straps, except for the winter aviation working overcoat and raincoats, which showed no rank insignia.

The same type of stripes was applied on the sleeves and on the shoulder straps. At the beginning of World War 2, the stripes were worn all around the cuff but later they were placed on the outside only, from seam to seam and, from 1 January 1944, only the shorter stripes were permitted on service dress.

Flag officers were distinguished by gold lace stripes 2 in (50 mm) in width, combined on the sleeves with $\frac{1}{2}$ in (13 mm) stripes and with silver anchor and stars upon the stripe on the shoulder straps. A narrower stripe, $\frac{1}{4}$ in (6.5 mm) wide, was worn in combination with larger ones by the Lieutenant Commander and Lieutenant (Junior Grade), and the narrow stripe on its own by the Aviation Cadet, although later during the war the latter started to wear the Line star instead of the stripe.

Shoulder straps were $2\frac{3}{8}$ in (60 mm) in width, covered with navy blue or black cloth according to uniform, with stripes and badges, as illustrated. When grey working uniforms were introduced, new slate grey shoulder straps were adopted which carried black lace stripes, black embroidered 5-pointed star or corps devices, black anchor and rank stars for the flag officers.

The rank of Admiral of the Fleet was introduced on 14 December 1944; the rank of Commodore, but not its pay grade, was suspended from 1899 to April 1943 and, during World War 2, there were two graduations of the Rear Admiral's rank: the Rear Admiral of the upper half received the pay of his rank while that of the lower half was on the pay grade of the Commodore.

The Line Officer was qualified in all respects for command at sea of a specified ship or class of ship while a Staff Officer belonged to a corps and wore the corps badge instead of the 5-pointed star. Flag officers not of the Line wore a minature corps badge upon the shank of the anchor on the shoulder straps and the corps badge above the cuff stripes, in place of the star. Flag officers of the U.S. Coast Guard had the shield upon the anchor.

The following were the corps and their respective badges:

Corps	Badge
Medical	Silver acorn and gold oak leaf
Dental	Gold oak leaf and two silver acorns
Supply	A sprig of three oak leaves with three acorns in gold
Chaplain { Christian	Inclined, gold Roman Cross
{ Jewish	Gold Star of David above the Tablets of the Law
Civil Engineering	Two gold sprigs of two live oak leaves and a silver acorn

Corps	Badge
Nurse	Gold foul anchor with oak leaf, acorn and silver initials superimposed
Band	Gold lyre

The U.S. Coast Guard was not a corps but a service in its own right with the Coast Guard Shield as its badge, in gold for officers and warrant officers, silver for the Chief Petty Officer and in white or dark blue according to uniform, for the enlisted men. Chief petty officers and enlisted men wore the shield on the right forearm of the jumper.

Nurses wore their badge on the collar and, as we have seen already, on the cap as well.

The corps badges, also called sleeve markings, were always embroidered when worn on the sleeves while those for the shoulder straps could be embroidered or made of metal. Smaller badges, about five-eighths the size of those mentioned above, were worn on the left side of the collar of the khaki shirt and, together with rank insignia for the shirt's collar, are illustrated on Plate 42.

Plate 42. Warrant Officers' Rank and Corps Insignia

The Chief Warrant Officer and Warrant Officer were distinguished by large and narrow broken stripes, respectively; i.e. gold stripes with intermittent blue segments. They had the corps badge above the stripe and on the collar of the khaki shirt and some had special rank titles: for instance, the Chief Warrant Officer who wore the crossed anchors device was known as Chief Boatswain, the Chief Gunner wore the bursting cannon grenade, and so on.

The following were the corps and their respective badges:

Corps	Badge
Boatswain	Crossed foul anchors
Gunner	Bursting cannon grenade
Carpenter	Carpenter's square
Ship's Clerk	Crossed quill pens
Torpedoman	Torpedo
Radio Electrician	Four zigzag rays of lightning
Machinist	3-bladed propeller
Electrician	Globe
Photographer	Camera
Pharmacist	Caduceus
Aerographer	Circle divided by an arrow
Pay Clerk	A sprig of three oak leaves

The warrant officers of the U.S. Coast Guard wore, on the sleeves and on the shoulder straps, the shield and the corps badge as illustrated.

Officers' Miniature Rank and Corps Insignia

Naval officers wore U.S. Army/Marine Corps type of rank insignia on the garrison cap and on the shirt collar of the khaki summer working uniform. These badges were smaller than those worn on the shoulder straps by personnel of the other two services and were attached by means of a pin; admirals' stars, when more than one, were attached one to the other. Officers of the Line had rank insignia on both sides of the collar while Officers of the Corps wore the rank insignia on the right side and a minature corps insignia on the left side of the collar.

All miniature corps badges were made of metal and were about five-eighths of the size of those used on the sleeves and shoulder straps. The officers' badges were made of gold metal.

The warrant officers wore their corps badges on the collar of the khaki summer shirt: the Chief Warrant Officer had silver badges, the Warrant Officer gold ones, made of plain metal and not intended to imitate embroidery. A version of the photographer's badge shows a front view of a camera.

Plate 43. Insignia for Petty Officers

The rating badge consisted basically of the eagle, chevrons, arc and speciality mark. The eagle and speciality mark were white and the chevrons and arc were red on a navy blue background for blue uniform, while all the devices were navy blue on a white background for wear on white uniform. Navy blue badges on slate grey were used on grey uniforms.

The Chief Petty Officer and Petty Officer with no less than 12 years' service, holding three consecutive good conduct awards or equivalent outstanding record, were entitled to gold chevrons and silver embroidered eagle and speciality mark on blue uniform. The Chief Petty Officer who did not qualify for gold chevrons wore the usual white and red insignia or, optionally, silver embroidered eagle and speciality mark, but always red chevrons and arc. The chief petty officers wore officers' type uniform while petty officers had sailors' uniform.

The personnel of the Seaman Branch had the rate badge on the upper right sleeve and those of the other branches on the left. Branch was identified by a stripe of braid $\frac{23}{64}$ in (9 mm) in width sewn all around the seam between the sleeve and the shoulder of the jumper; Seaman Branch was shown by a stripe along the right shoulder, white for blue jumper and blue for white jumper, while the other branches, commonly known as Fireman Branch, displayed a red stripe on the left shoulder, regardless of the colour of the jumper.

Initially the eagle of the rate insignia faced to its left; thus the eagle of those who wore the badge on the left arm faced backward, but during the war it was decided that the eagle should always face forward of the wearer, regardless of its position on the uniform.

Service stripes, each representing 4 years of service were worn on the left forearm by those entitled. They were red for blue uniform and blue for white uniform. Three consecutive good conduct awards entitled the holder to gold service stripes on blue uniform.

Cuff Markings

The newly recruited sailor usually became an Apprentice Seaman and wore a single white stripe on both cuffs of the jumper; later he graduated to Seaman 2nd Class with two stripes, or Fireman 3rd Class, retaining in this case the single stripe, in accordance with his branch mark, i.e. Seaman Branch if he had a white stripe along the right shoulder seam, Fireman if he had a red one on the left shoulder. The cuff stripes were $\frac{7}{32}$ in (5 mm) in width and the double and treble cuff markings were joined together by vertical stripes; the whole insignia was about $4\frac{3}{4}$ in (120 mm) long.

Two coloured shoulder sleeve insignia complete this plate, that of the Construction Battalions, nicknamed 'Seebees', and of the Minecraft Personnel.

Plate 44. Cap Tallies

Petty officers and non-rated enlisted men wore two types of cloth head-dress, the navy blue nicknamed 'Donald Duck' cap and the white hat with folded-up brim.

The former displayed a black tally with 'U.S. NAVY' or 'U.S. COAST GUARD' titles, according to service, while the latter did not show any insignia.

Speciality Marks

These badges have been illustrated in navy blue on a white background, as worn as part of rating insignia or on their own on the white uniform.

Speciality marks were introduced in 1841, starting with the crossed anchors of the Boatswain; many marks later disappeared or were changed to a new design following the development of tasks and specialisations on ships. The marks illustrated are those in use during World War 2. Many others were adopted later, during the last 30 years.

Marks whose title included the word 'Mate' indicated that the career in the speciality advanced up to the rank of Warrant Officer; thus the rating assisted his warrant officer in that particular job.

The badges were dark blue for white uniforms and of white or silver embroidery for blue uniform, except for the red cross of the Hospital Apprentice—Pharmacist Mate, which was red for all uniforms.

Most marks, and the job they represented, are self explanatory but some brief additional notes could still help the reader to understand better this rather difficult subject.

There was no Boatswain's Mate 3rd Class as this rate was known by the title of Coxswain; duties included the steering of ships and handling of boats, with knowledge of signals, charting of compass courses, directing salvage operations, etc. The Quartermasters' duties included the steering of ships, signalling by semaphore or blinker searchlight, etc. general navigation, the taking of soundings, the use of the rangefinder—a variety of jobs which had nothing in common with those of the army counterpart.

Aerographers dealt with meteorological observation and the Fire Controlman, who wore the gun's rangefinder as his badge, controlled the firing of the ship's gun. The Soundman's badge depicted earphones with an arrow across. The Chief Commissary Steward was always a Chief Petty Officer and his lower ratings were Baker and Cook, whose badge was the crescent moon with horizontal stripes below. The rate of Chief Officers' Steward or Cook was adopted in 1942; the rate badges of the Messman Branch, later redesignated Steward Branch, have been illustrated as worn on blue uniform.

Plate 45. Distinguishing Marks and Specialist Ratings

Distinguishing marks identified special qualifications attained by non-rated men or ratings, but in addition to the qualifications shown by the speciality mark.

Although distinguishing marks were usually worn above or below the elbow on either sleeve, the positioning was specified in each case. The Ex-Apprentice badge, for instance, was worn by the Chief Petty Officer below the rating badge and by the petty officers on the breast of the jumper, below the loop that held the neckerchief.

As usual the badge was white for blue uniform and blue for white uniform except the 'E' for Excellence in Engineering which was always red. Second and further awards of an 'E' in gunnery or engineering were identified by one or more small bars under the original badge.

Many badges illustrated as speciality marks were initially used as distinguishing marks by non-rated enlisted men. These are the following which are not shown again for lack of space:

Qualification	**Badge**
Quartermaster	Ship's wheel
Storekeeper	Crossed keys
Signalman	Crossed flags
Radioman	Lightning sparks

Qualification	Badge
Boilermaker	3-bladed propeller
Electrician's Mate	Globe
Gunner's Mate	Crossed cannons
Musician	Lyre
Yeoman	Crossed quill pens
Torpedoman's Mate	Torpedo
Aerographer's Mate	Circle divided by an arrow
Gun Range Finder Operator	Rangefinder

The Fire Controlman and the Gun Range Finder Operator wore the same badge but the former's was a speciality mark and the latter's a distinguishing mark.

The specialist ratings and their corresponding specialities were introduced during the war and all depicted letters of the alphabet, about $\frac{5}{8}$ in (16 mm) in height, enclosed in a diamond-shaped frame; specialists were eligible for ratings.

The letter 'I' stood for International Business Machine Operator, later changed to Punched-card Accounting Machine Operator. The initials 'PT' identified the PTC Motor Torpedo Boats' specialists. In 1943, the frame was dropped from the badge of the Construction Battalions.

Initially about a dozen specialists' badges were adopted, followed by more and more until, eventually, even an 'X' badge appeared for individuals who had no specific qualification.

Many of these badges, as well as speciality and distinguishing marks, were used also by the U.S. Coast Guard.

Plate 46. Qualification Badges

The Naval Aviator wings were adopted at the beginning of 1919 and were used during World War 2 by pilots of the U.S. Navy, Marine Corps and Coast Guard. The Aviation Observer badge appeared in 1922 as a one-winged device, which, in 1927, developed into the Balloon Observer badge which was later redesignated Balloon Pilot badge. The wings of the Naval Aviation Observer were finally introduced in 1929.

The Flight Surgeon badge was the next to be introduced, followed, in 1944, by the Air Crew Insignia, with stars above it in a scroll, to show the number of engagements in which the wearer had taken part, namely air combat, action against enemy ships or fortified positions on the ground. No more than three stars could be applied on to the badge which, incidentally, could be used by officers and enlisted men not eligible for other aviation wings.

The badges of the Tactical Observer, Navigator and Radar Observer were adopted later during the war. Smaller wings, about half the size of the normal ones, were worn by officers on the evening dress and white mess jacket.

There were three types of submarine badges: for officers, for surgeons and the Combat Insignia. The latter was awarded to officers and men who completed one or more missions in which the submarine sank at least one enemy vessel or accomplished a combat mission of equal importance. The officers wore it below their ribbons.

A badge similar to that of the submarine's officers, but embroidered, was worn by enlisted men as a distinguishing mark on the right forearm.

Miscellanea

Personnel on Shore Patrol duty wore a navy blue armlet, $3\frac{15}{16}$ in (100 mm) wide, with large yellow 'SP' initials on the upper sleeve opposite the rating badge. The Geneva Cross armlet was always worn on the right upper arm.

The Honorable Discharge badge depicted the American Eagle in a circle, the whole embroidered in yellow on cloth matching the colour of the uniform, and was worn on the right breast.

The shoulder sleeve insignia of Amphibious Forces, depicting the interallied emblem of combined operation, in gold on red background for the navy, was worn on the upper left sleeve, below the shoulder seam.

Women members of the Women's Reserve of the U.S. Naval Reserve were known as W.A.V.E.S. while members of the Women's Reserve of the U.S. Coast Guard Reserve were called S.P.A.R.S. Officers of both organisations wore the male officers' cap badge on their distinctive hats while the enlisted women had naval or Coast Guard tallies instead.

Naval female officers had special collar badges depicting a white anchor on a blue propeller, the whole on a navy blue circular background. The Shore Establishment device was worn on both sides of the collar by S.P.A.R.S.; officers and enlisted women wore the Coast Guard Shield on the sleeves according to usual custom.

Both W.A.V.E.S. and S.P.A.R.S. officers wore rank stripes of 'reserve' blue instead of gold on the sleeves but no shoulder boards and both used distinctive shoulder bags of the same pattern.

The personnel of the U.S. Marine Corps Women's Reserve wore the same badges as their male counterparts and brown leather shoulder bags of special pattern.

Gilt buttons were used by officers and warrant officers of the U.S. Navy; they depicted the eagle perched on the shaft of the anchor encircled by thirteen stars. Large black buttons displaying the foul anchor were used by enlisted men on the overcoat and smaller ones with 'NAVY' above the anchor were worn on the dungarees. The officers' cooks and stewards had small black buttons, the anchor without rope, on the jacket of the blue uniform and the same type of button, but smaller, was worn by all enlisted men on the trousers.

The Coast Guards' button for officers and warrant officers had a straight eagle perched on top of the anchor and a laurel and oak leaves wreath. Enlisted men used black U.S. Navy buttons.

Marines had gilt and bronze buttons according to uniform; the button displayed the eagle perched on top of the anchor, with the thirteen stars placed around the top half of the button's edge.

Plate 47. U.S.M.C. Head-dress and Collar, Corps and Rank Insignia

The emblem of the U.S. Marine Corps, adopted in 1868, displayed the American Eagle above the globe, which is superimposed upon a foul anchor, with a scroll above the whole device that depicts the corps motto *Semper Fidelis*.

The latter scroll is not shown on insignia worn on uniform. Large badges made of metal were worn on the peaked cap, smaller ones on the garrison cap and on the collar. The officers' large badge had a separate rope, in imitation of a real rope, which was twisted in place around the anchor, while the rope of the enlisted men's badges was struck as part of the badge and therefore the spaces between the anchor and the rope were not cut out.

The badges used by officers on the blue and the white dress caps were made of silver and gilt, enlisted men's dress cap badges were made of brass, while the badges used on service dress, by both officers and enlisted men, were made of bronze, differing by their rope, as mentioned above.

The badge used on the garrison cap and on the collar had no rope at all; the former were always made of bronze while the collar badges matched the cap badge, i.e. with variations in silver and gilt, brass and bronze, according to type of uniform. Collar badges were worn in pairs with the anchors facing inward; the garrison cap badge was worn on the left side of the cap with its centre at $1\frac{31}{32}$ in (50 mm) from the front.

Aviation cadets wore a winged propeller in bronze or silver and gilt but, eventually, their training was taken on by the U.S. Navy, thus they came to wear naval uniforms and became part of the U.S.M.C. on receiving commission.

All officers had a cross-shaped ornament made of braid on the top of the peaked cap; the braid matched the colour of the cap. The permanent staff officers of departments and the aides-de-camp used special badges on the lapels of the service jacket and behind the U.S.M.C. device on the standing collar of the blue and the white tunic.

Service dress badges were made of bronze, while the badges for blue or white uniforms were made of silver and gilt and, except for the badge of the Adjutant and Inspector's Department, they had a coloured enamel finish.

The insignia of the Adjutant and Inspector's Department depicted a shield surrounded by a laurel wreath upon a sword crossed with fasces; the same badge was worn on the right and on the left side of the collar, while the following other badges were worn in pairs.

The badge of the Paymasters' Department depicted a sprig of oak leaves on a red tablet, encircled by an oak leaves wreath superimposed upon a sword crossed with a quill pen. A wheel with thirteen spokes and thirteen stars on a blue enamelled rim, superimposed on crossed sword and key, was the badge of the Quartermasters' Department.

The Aides-de-Camp wore, on the collar, the eagle above the shield, with one or more stars on the latter according to the number of stars of the general whom the officer was supposed to aid.

The officers of the Marine Corps used rank insignia of army type: generals had silver stars, the Colonel an eagle, the Lieutenant Colonel and Major silver or gold oak leaves, respectively, and the company officers displayed rectangular metal bars, the 2nd Lieutenant one only, made of gold.

In 1942 the Commandant of the Marine Corps was upgraded to the rank of Lieutenant General and later to the rank of General, with four stars.

Shoulder straps of jackets, tunics and overcoats of the U.S.M.C. differed from those of the other services in so far as they had rounded ends instead of pointed ends, as illustrated.

Plate 48. U.S.M.C. Warrant Officers' Rank and Corps Insignia

The U.S. Marine Corps had two warrant officers who wore departmental badges like the officers, plus the gunner's grenade and the lyre of the Second Leader of the Marine Band.

The commissioned Chief Warrant Officer, later redesignated Commissioned Warrant Officer was known simply as 'Chief' and wore as rank insignia a gold bar with a blue band across its centre. Departmental chiefs had special titles: Chief Marine Gunner, Chief Pay Clerk, Chief Quartermaster Clerk and the chief of the Adjutant and Inspector's Department was known as Chief Quartermaster Clerk (A. and I.) to distinguish him from the chief of the Quartermasters' Department.

Chief warrant officers wore the Marine Corps badge and departmental chief warrant officers and gunners wore their appropriate badge as well on the collar of jackets and tunics and rank insignia on the shoulder straps, as did the officers. However, on the overcoat and raincoat, they had the departmental device or the grenade as well as the rank insignia on both shoulder straps.

The Warrant Officer wore only the departmental device in lieu of rank insignia on the shoulder straps. The 2nd Leader of the Marine Band wore a silver lyre on all uniforms while all the other chiefs and warrant officers had bronze badges on service uniform and 'dress' badges on blue and on white uniforms. The Leader of the Marine Band was an officer.

Miniature rank insignia, departmental badges, the grenade and the lyre were worn on the collar of the khaki summer shirt in accordance with usual custom.

Distinguishing Marks

Four naval distinguishing marks could be awarded to marines and were worn on the right forearm of dress blue and service uniforms, centred between the elbow and the bottom of the sleeve, except for the 'E', which was placed at $2\frac{1}{2}$ in (63 mm) above the bottom edge of the sleeve.

The badges were red on blue or khaki cloth background, according to uniform.

Shoulder Sleeve Insignia—1st Marine Amphibious Corps

Cloth patches were seldom granted to the marines and, in March 1943 only, the Commandant of the Marine Corps authorised the wearing of a limited number of shoulder sleeve insignia, starting with the insignia of the 1st Division; others were adopted later.

The 1st Marine Amphibious Corps was identified by a rather large blue patch in the shape of a square shield, depicting the constellation of the Southern Cross and a red diamond in the centre which identified the deployment or specialisation of its wearer.

The plain red diamond was used by anti-tank units, the $6\frac{1}{8}$ in (155 mm) Howitzer Battalion and all corps personnel, except those who were part of the following units which had special badges in the diamond:

Units	Badge
Balloon Barrage Battalions	Captive balloon
Defence Battalions	Anti-aircraft gun
Paratroopers	Open parachute
Raiders	Skull
Service & Supply	5-pointed star

Later, artillerymen were granted the crossed cannons in the diamond.

All shoulder patches were worn on the upper left sleeve, below the shoulder seam.

Plate 49. U.S.M.C. N.C.O.s' Rank Insignia

The U.S. marines used three types of chevrons: gold on a red background for the dress blue uniform, green (dark khaki) on red for the green winter uniform and black on light khaki for the summer shirt.

The non-commissioned officers of the Line had chevrons joined by arcs while those of the Staff had theirs joined by ties, i.e. straight stripes.

The marine advanced into the Line or Staff careers by becoming a Private 1st Class (6th Grade) but only when he reached the 3rd Grade rank did the arc or tie identify the branch to which he belonged. Aviation N.C.O.s wore ties under their chevrons as aviation was one of the specialisations of Staff.

The branches were: Line, Music, Signals and Radio, Quartermaster, Paymaster, Aviation and Mess.

The lozenge within the First Sergeant's badge was adopted during World War 2, while the badge with three chevrons and three arcs was worn by the Sergeant Major and Master Gunnery Sergeant (1st Grade Line). The First Sergeant was quoted as the leading man in his company while the other two were experts in their own trades: the Sergeant Major in drills, regulations, billeting and administration and the Master Gunnery Sergeant in arms and ordnance.

The 1st Grade Staff covered the ranks of Master Technical, Quartermaster and Paymaster Sergeant and there were no rank insignia with the lozenge in the Staff branches. The Gunnery Sergeant (2nd Grade Line) wore three chevrons and two arcs while the Technical Sergeant, Drum Major and Supply Sergeant (2nd Grade Staff) had three chevrons and two ties. The Platoon Sergeant (3rd Grade Line) and the Staff Sergeant (3rd Grade Staff) wore three chevrons and one arc, or tie, respectively. The Sergeant (4th Grade), Corporal (5th Grade) and Private 1st Class (6th Grade) wore three, two and one chevron, and the Private (7th Grade) had no rank insignia at all.

There were five grades of musician: Principal Musician with rank insignia corresponding to the 2nd Grade; 1st, 2nd, 3rd Class Musician and Private 1st Class, all with the lyre below the chevrons. Later the whole system was changed with the creation of the rank of Band Leader, wearing three chevrons, three arcs and the lyre, and of Musician with one chevron, one arc and the lyre.

Until September 1942 chevrons were worn on both upper sleeves, later on the left sleeve alone.

Service stripes, each corresponding to 4 years of service, were worn on the outer part of the forearm of the left sleeve in colours matching the colour of the chevrons.

Plate 50. U.S.M.C. Shoulder Sleeve Insignia—Amphibious Corps

The first corps patch to be adopted for the Amphibious Corps, Pacific Fleet, later became the insignia of the 5th Marine Amphibious Corps, and the three stars on the badge stand for the rank insignia of a Lieutenant General, a corps commander.

The patch of the 3rd Marine amphibious Corps depicted the mythological sea monster Leviathan of the Scriptures, below the corps' number in Roman figures. The head of an alligator below three white stars was the emblem of the 5th Corps, formerly Amphibious Corps, as already mentioned.

Divisions

The 'Guadalcanal Blaze' of the 1st Marine Division was the first divisional insignia adopted during World War 2 and was designed by Lieutenant Colonel M. B. Twining, U.S.M.C., who served in the division as operations officer at Guadalcanal. Appropriately the badge depicts the figure '1', inscribed 'Guadalcanal', upon the constellation of the Southern Cross, on a blue background.

The patch of the 2nd Marine Division followed in style that of the former, with a figure '2', in the form of a snake, inscribed with the same battle honour. This badge was superseded by another pattern, showing a hand holding a torch and the Southern Cross, the whole on an arrowhead-shaped red background.

A 3-pointed star device on an equilateral curvilinear red triangle became the badge of the 3rd Marine Division and the figure '4', on a red diamond, the badge of the 4th Marine Division. The 5th Marine Division's badge displayed a blue arrowhead which symbolises the marines' role of relentless attack, upon a 'V', which stands for Victory and for its numerical designation, the whole on a red shield. Three battle honours were shown in the badge of the 6th Marine Division: 'Melanesia' referred to the islands northeast of Australia; 'Micronesia' to the islands of the West Pacific, including the Marianas, Carolinas, Marshall, Palao and Gilbert Islands, and the battle honour 'Orient' was selected because the 4th Marine Regiment, lost in Bataan and later reactivated as part of the 6th Division, came from China, and in anticipation that the final stages of the war would be fought in the Orient.

The marines serving in Londonderry, Northern Ireland, adopted a patch which combined the Marine Corps emblem and the Irish shamrock, a fine badge which however remained unofficial and was eventually discarded.

Defence Units

The defense battalions were deployed as anti-aircraft units: the 13th Defense Battalion's patch carried a seahorse while the other three battalions' badges displayed emblems symbolic of their deployment, a sword upon wings in the case of the 18th and anti-aircraft guns for the other two.

There were two variants of the Ship Detachments' patch: with blue or with black anchor under the seahorse.

The patch of the 4th Marine Base Defense Air Wing showed the figure '4' above an eagle poised to drop a bomb. The unit was formed in August 1942 and, in November 1944, it joined the 4th Aircraft Wing.

Plate 51. U.S.M.C. Shoulder Sleeve Insignia—Fleet Marine Forces

Some rather large shield-shaped patches, embroidered in yellow and white on a red background, were used by the Fleet Marine Forces. The central device identified the assignment of the wearer, i.e. a fist holding four lightnings for headquarters, an anti-aircraft gun for anti-aircraft personnel, a field gun for artillery, etc.

Aircraft Wings

Aviation personnel wore special patches based on the design of the aircraft fuselage insignia, with yellow stars, wings and a Roman number below, which refers to the wing's number. The headquarters' emblem displayed a Spanish crown, which stands for California where it was organised.

Later these shield-shaped badges were replaced by kite-shaped ones, somehow simplified in their symbolism: all depicted a winged Marine Corps emblem with the unit's designation below.

Plate 52. Subsidiary Services

The personnel of some subsidiary services which, incidentally had little or nothing in common with the U.S. Navy, wore navy-blue uniforms and used insignia of naval type; it may be useful therefore to show at least some specimens of their badges.

The Army Transport Service was redesignated during the war as Army Transportation Corps Vessels and was supervised by the Water Division of Transportation Corps, Army Service Forces. It shared its badges with another subsidiary organisation, the Harbor Boat Service. Their personnel had special rank designation identified on uniform by gold, silver or lustrous black stripes, often on branch colours, according to rank or speciality on the cuffs and shoulder marks. Port officials had white braid on white uniforms and brown on khaki uniforms.

The officers' cap badge depicted the American Eagle with enamelled shield on the breast, perched on crossed anchors. The Marine Superintentent and Superintending Engineer wore, on the collar, the initials 'A.T.S.' upon the ship's steering wheel with thirteen stars on the rim; the other officers wore the initials only in gold, the stewards only in silver. The following branch badges were worn on the lapels

Badge	Designation of Task
Foul anchor in gold	Marine Superintendent, Master, Chief Stevedore, Deck Officers, A.T.S. and Master, Mate, Pilot, H.B.S.

Designation of Task	Badge
3-bladed propeller in gold	Superintending Engineer, Engineering Officers, A.T.S. and Chief and Assistant Engineer, H.B.S.
Insignia of Transportation Corps in gold	Transportation Agent
Crossed quill pens in gold	Clerks on piers and on transports
Five lightnings in gold	Radioman, civilian
Crescent in silver	Steward

Personnel of the A.T.S. and H.B.S. had the initials above the foul anchor on their gold buttons, stewards wore silver buttons.

The petty officers wore, on the peaked cap, a branch badge or the designation of task surrounded by a wreath, as follows:

Badge	Task
Crossed anchors	Boatswain
Crossed batons	Master at Arms and Assistant
Crossed axes	Carpenter
Ship's steering wheel with stars on blue enamel rim	Wheelman
3-bladed propeller	Machinist, Refrigerating Engineer, Deck Engineer, Chief Electrician, Plumber, Boilermaker, Water Tender and their Assistants

and the following designation of task in place of the badge: Yeoman, Storekeeper, Assistant Storekeeper, Baggagemaster, Porter, Watchman and Barber.

Ratings wore from one to three red chevrons above the red branch badge on a blue background, as illustrated.

U.S. Maritime Service

The insignia of the Maritime Service followed the U.S. Navy pattern and its personnel used the rank insignia and rank-rate designation of the navy. The officers graduated up to the rank of Vice Admiral and wore gold lace stripes on the cuffs and shoulder marks below corps devices, surrounded by a gold wreath. The device, or emblem, of Line was the foul anchor; the others were the same as those of the U.S. Navy, for Supply, Hospital Corps, Radio Electrician and Chaplains.

The warrant officers used navy devices as well, all except those of Gunner,

Torpedoman and Aerographer and, like their officers, wore them enclosed in a wreath.

The petty officers had red chevrons and speciality marks of naval type below a red anchor combined with the initials 'USMS'.

U.S. Coast and Geodetic Survey

The emblem of this organisation depicted a silver globe with a gold triangle in its centre, which suggests the triangulation methods used in geodetic surveys.

It was worn by all commissioned officers above the rank stripes on the cuffs and shoulder marks, with the exception of the commandant, a Rear Admiral, who had the device superimposed upon a foul anchor on his shoulder marks, and the device alone on the cuffs.

Civil service ships' officers graduated as Chief Engineer, Surgeon, Mate or Deck Officer and wore a 3-bladed propeller, the naval hospital device or binoculars respectively, instead of the globe and triangle. The Deck Officer had no insignia.

Ratings wore chevrons like naval ratings except that the eagle of the U.S.C. & G.S. was perched on the top segment of a globe; chief petty officers with 12 years' meritorious service had gold chevrons and arc. The following speciality badges were used:

Speciality	**Badge**
Boatswain	Foul anchor
Yeoman	Crossed quill pens
Carpenter	Axe
Radio Technician	Lightnings
Oiler	3-bladed propeller
Coxwain	Fouled arrow
Electrician	Armature
Quartermaster	Steering wheel
Master at Arms	Shield
Pharmacist	Red cross
Officers' Steward or Cook	Crescent

The cap badges of officers and Chief Petty Officer have been illustrated; the latter is similar to the badge worn by the Rear Admiral on the shoulder marks. The officers' stewards and cooks wore on the cap the initials 'US' above 'C&GS' and, like their counterparts of the navy, had bars instead of chevrons as rate insignia.

Petty officers and seamen wore the white hat or blue cap, the latter with the tally illustrated.

U.S. Public Health Service

The emblem of this organisation is a winged caduceus superimposed on a horizontal foul anchor, the former signifying medicine and the latter a sailor in distress.

This emblem was part of the cap badge and on its own was worn on the garrison cap, above rank stripes on cuffs and shoulder marks and as a lapel badge on olive drab army type uniforms. The rank titles of the Public Health Service corresponded with those of the army and navy medical corps and were displayed in naval style on uniforms or in army style on olive drab uniforms, according to assignment.

The P.H.S.'s emblem was used as a corps device, as follows:

Corps	**Badge**
Medical and Engineer Officers	The emblem
Acting Assistant Surgeon	With additional 'A'
Dental Officers	With additional 'D'
Scientific Officer	With additional 'S'

Additional badges were worn above the corps badges by:

Intern at Marine Hospitals	Aesculapius staff
Pharmacist	Winged caduceus
Administrative Assistant	Crossed key and pen
Chaplain	Roman Cross

Cadet nurses in training wore a special grey uniform with beret and displayed a special shoulder sleeve insignia on the left upper arm.

Japan

The Japanese started to organise a modern fleet in the middle of the last century with the help of Dutch experts, as initially they had bought some ships from Holland. Later, British expertise and influence took over and, by 1894, the Japanese defeated the Chinese fleet. The Russo-Japanese War of 1904–05 marked another Japanese success and, later, the advance continued into China.

All was made possible by the raising of a powerful and efficient navy. The first major modernisation of uniforms took place in 1884 and, although many changes took place later, those first dress regulations established the standards of uniforms and badges for the next 50 years.

Uniforms became more practical, and insignia less decorative, as the Imperial Japanese Navy became progressively more engaged farther and farther from its homeland.

Plate 53. Cap Badges

The officers wore, on the peaked cap, a gold anchor in a ring surrounded by a gold wreath, the whole ensigned by a silver cherry blossom; the petty officers wore the cherry blossom superimposed upon the anchor with an oval gold edge around it and the midshipmen had a gold foul anchor alone.

The cherry blossom upon the anchor was worn by officers and ratings, except seamen, on the field cap; the latter wore a plain anchor. There were several variations of both these badges as the colour of the emblem and its background changed according to the colour of the cap. Some badges were embroidered in gold, others in yellow or blue thread, others woven in silk.

The cap tally of the sailors had swallow's tail-shaped ends and a yellow anchor on both sides.

Plates 53, 54 and 55. Officers' Rank Insignia

The naval officers had the same rank titles as the officers of the army, the former's title was preceded by the term 'Kaigun' (Navy) and the latter's by 'Rikugun' (Army) in order to distinguish between the services.

Rank distinction was shown in the form of gold lace stripes with curl on the cuffs of the blue dress uniform and overcoat, black lace stripes on the service dress tunic and, in the latter's case, additional collar patches. The service dress tunic had black lace trimmings along the top and front edge of the collar, the front and skirt and on the pockets.

The flag officers had two large stripes with one, two or three medium stripes above, the uppermost with the curl, and the other officers used medium stripes; the Lieutenant-Commander's and Sub-Lieutenant's combined with a narrow one (which, on its own, was used by midshipmen and cadets), the former with the curl and the latter without it.

Only some examples of cuff stripes are shown, but all the shoulder straps for each rank have been illustrated.

Shoulder straps were intended for use on the white tunic but were often worn on blue and khaki tunics as well. They were shaped in a particular manner, typical of all Japanese epaulettes and shoulder straps and carried gold lace stripes, which distinguished class of rank, and silver cherry blossoms to identify individual ranks.

The Midshipman wore the stripe of the junior officers' class without the cherry blossom device and the Cadet had a gold anchor on plain blue shoulder straps.

The collar patches were made of navy blue cloth, with gold stripes and silver cherry blossoms, as on the shoulder straps, and were worn on the blue service uniform, khaki jackets and shirts.

Only cherry blossom devices were worn on the collar of the cape and identified class of rank: three cherry blossoms were worn by flag officers, two by senior officers and one by junior officers.

Officers who were commissioned from the ranks were identified by different badges, as illustrated; they could graduate to the rank of Lieutenant and had three gold cherry blossoms below the usual navy cuff stripes. They had silver cherry blossoms on the shoulder straps but above a narrower gold lace stripe, of warrant officer's width.

The rank insignia of non-executive officers have been illustrated on Plate 58. The corps were identified by coloured distinction cloth placed as a background to the cuff stripes, on both sides of the gold lace on the shoulder straps and as longitudinal piping on the collar patches. Midshipmen and cadets of the corps wore a coloured anchor on the cap.

The following were the corps and their corresponding colours:

Corps	**Colour**
Engineers	Violet
Ship and Engine Constructors	Brown
Ordnance Constructors	Purple-brown
Medical	Red
Legal	Pale green
Paymasters	White
Survey Officers	Black
Aviation Officers and Hydrographers	Light blue
Chief Carpenters (Warrant Officer)	Green
Bandmaster (Warrant Officer)	Grey-blue

During the course of the war, gold or dark blue stripes, according to the colour of the cap badge, were adopted for wear on the field cap, all around its base, below the badge. These stripes identified class of rank: three stripes for flag officers, two for senior officers and one for junior officers.

Cuff stripes of reduced version were adopted as well, for practical reasons. The stripes and curl were sewn on a square patch of dark blue cloth and, as such, could be worn on the breast or on the upper sleeve of special field uniforms or overalls.

In January 1944, the conventional rank insignia on the cuffs were changed to three, two or one narrow gold stripes without curl, according to class of rank, with three, two or one gold cherry blossoms below, according to rank.

Plate 56, 57. Petty Officers' and Seamen's Rate Badges (1st type)

Petty officers and seamen at first wore their rate and corps devices combined on the upper sleeves. The badges were round in shape and displayed red devices on dark blue background for wear on blue uniform, blue devices on white for white uniform.

The petty officers were identified by a wreath on the badges; the Petty Officer 1st Class and Seaman 1st Class wore crossed corps devices ensigned by a cherry blossom, those of 2nd Class wore crossed devices without the cherry blossom and those of 3rd Class had a single corps device in the badge.

The design of several badges was modified during the war, as for instance the device of the Aviation Corps, illustrated, and new ones were added.

Red or blue Good Conduct chevrons, according to uniform, were worn above the badge; chevrons with a small cherry blossom at the apex identified Excellent Conduct.

Midshipmen and cadets of the navy wore the anchor on the collar and, later, a winged cherry blossom was adopted instead for those of the naval aviation.

Plate 58. Good Conduct Chevrons, Petty Officers' and Seamen's Rate Insignia (2nd Type)

The second pattern of rate badges was yellow and only the background was changed to match the colour of the uniform. All displayed an anchor, on its own for seamen and surrounded by a wreath for petty officers, ensigned by a cherry blossom in corps colour. Three, two or one yellow bar above the cherry blossom identified the specific class of rating, although the rates' titles by then had been altered to include the Seaman 2nd Class who wore the anchor and cherry blossom without any bar.

Later, the definitive graduation included the Leading Seaman, who wore three bars, the Superior Seaman with two, the Seaman 1st Class with one bar, and the Seaman 2nd Class.

Ratings of the Line had yellow cherry blossom in the badge while those of the other corps used the colours previously listed. The badge was worn on the right upper sleeve, below eventual Good or Excellent Conduct chevrons, as before, but now yellow. A larger cherry blossom device, in two versions, as illustrated, was worn on the left upper sleeve by those who had attained special training qualifications.

Poland

The modern Polish Navy was created after World War 1 but it has a long history that goes back to the years before the partitions of the eighteenth century. Danzig became a naval base in the mid-sixteenth century and its ships destroyed a Swedish squadron in 1627; later, King Władysław IV strengthened the navy and constructed a fortified base on the Hel Peninsula.

However, Poland was mainly engaged in land warfare due to its geographical position in the centre of Europe; thus it never became a sea-faring power and never had colonies overseas.

After World War 1, Poland became the possessor of a narrow strip of land on the Baltic and a naval base was constructed at Gdynia, and became active in 1924. In the following years, Poland had some ships built in France but, by the late 1930s, it had its own arsenal and shipyard at Gdynia, where minesweepers were built and later two destroyers laid down.

On 28 August 1939, on the basis of an agreement between the Polish Naval Staff and the British Admiralty, three Polish destroyers, *Grom*, *Błyskawica* and *Burza*, left Gdynia and arrived in Britain, where they were met by the destroyer H.M.S. *Wallace*, on 1 September, on the first day of the war.

Plate 59. Cap and Rank Insignia

The first naval dress regulations, the Order No. 5 dated 18 January 1919, prescribed infantry type of uniforms with light blue and white piping and additional foul anchor on cap badges and shoulder straps.

At that time, many sailors came to the Polish Navy after having served in foreign navies, namely the Austrian, Russian and German Navy, and still wore foreign uniforms. Due to lack of supplies, they probably continued to wear those uniforms but with Polish insignia.

The first comprehensive dress regulations which introduced dark blue and white uniforms appeared in 1920 and were subsequently modified by several orders, the last one dated 9 December 1936.

The officers' blue and white caps had a gold and silver embroidered badge, black leather chin strap and visor which displayed the wearer's rank in the form of gold stars applied on to the former and stripes on the visor. The flag officers had a 'zigzag', the senior officers a double stripe and the junior officers a single stripe.

Officers wore gold lace stripes on the cuffs of the blue jacket and the same stripes on the shoulder straps of the white jacket and overcoat. The flag officers used large gold lace stripes, twisted to form a zigzag, surmounted by one, two or three narrow stripes with curl, according to rank. The senior officers had the large stripe, straight, in place of the zigzag and the junior officers wore the narrow stripes alone.

The dress belt was made of leather, covered on the outside by gold lace with two woven blue stripes and lined on the inside by navy blue velvet. A plain black leather belt could be used with the same buckle, which displayed the same emblem present on the buttons.

Plate 60. Cap and Rank Insignia

Gold metal stars could be fixed directly on to the chin strap or were embroidered in gold wire on a small patch of black cloth, and slipped on the chin strap.

Distinction cloth identified the naval branches and was worn as a backing to the officers' rank stripes, showing in between the stripes or below the one stripe rank. The following were the branches of the Polish Navy and their distinguishing colours:

Branch	**Distinction Cloth**
Line	—
Medical	Cherry red
Legal	Raspberry red
Technical	Green
Administration	Brown
River/Coastal	Light blue
Band	White

Doctors, advocates of the Legal Branch, musicians and administrative officers usually came from the army as they did not need training for executive naval command.

The officer cadets wore officers' uniforms and the chief petty officers' peaked cap and were eligible to ratings' chevrons and stripes but not to trade badges. They were distinguished by a gold metal badge, depicting a 5-pointed star surrounded by a laurel wreath which was later abolished.

Reserve officer cadets used piping of white and red twisted cords as their own distinction: ratings of 'A' category used it around the cuffs of the blue jacket and as piping to the shoulder straps, and those of 'B' category at a distance of $\frac{13}{32}$ in (10 mm) all around their stripes on the upper left sleeve.

The Warrant Officer and chief petty officers ('B' Category) wore gold chevrons, $\frac{15}{32}$ in (12 mm) in width, the former above a $\frac{8}{32}$ in (7 mm) stripe on both cuffs; chevrons and stripe were sewn on a backing of red felt which protruded all around the edges.

The Warrant Officer used the officers' type of cap badge while the others had their own pattern: a silver embroidered eagle with gold crown, perched on a blue 'Amazon' shield with a gold foul anchor in its centre, the whole on an oval felt background.

The Chief Petty Officer ('Bosman') was promoted to Chief Petty Officer 1st Class ('Starszy Bosman'—Senior Boatswain) after 6 years of service with good conduct.

Plate 61. Cap, Rate and Trade Insignia

Warrant and chief petty officers wore the gold trade badge on the left upper sleeve at $2\frac{3}{8}$–$2\frac{3}{4}$ in (60–70 mm) below the shoulder seam; the trade badge was not worn on the white jacket, nor on the work jacket.

The 'SP' initials stand for 'Szkoła Podchorążych' and, like the badge of the reserve cadets, was made of brass; both were similar to the cadets' badges of the army but the latter were made of white metal instead.

The junior ratings ('A' Category) wore a metal badge on the sailor's hat, at the front above the tally: the eagle and shield were made of white metal and the anchor of brass.

Rate was identified by one, two or three gold stripes on the left upper sleeve, at $1\frac{3}{16}$ in (30 mm) below the trade badge or, when lacking the trade badge, at $1\frac{3}{32}$–$6\frac{5}{16}$ in (150–160 mm) below the shoulder seam. The stripes were sewn on a red backing, like those of the senior ratings.

Plate 62. Cap Tallies and Trade Badges

The tallies were made of black silk and displayed the ship's name or the general title 'Marynarka Wojenna' in yellow letters.

The trade badges were self-explanatory, in red on a navy blue background. The first set of badges was adopted in 1920 and included crossed signallers' flags, crossed cannons, a flaming grenade, etc. others were added and modified later in accordance with the development of the service and progress of modern specialisations. Non-qualified seamen wore a plain foul anchor.

The Free Polish Navy in Great Britain

The three Polish destroyers in British ports were joined by the submarines *Wilk* and *Orzel* and, later, the training ships *Wilia* and *Iskra* turned up at Casablanca. In May 1940, the Royal Navy ceded H.M.S. *Garland* to the Polish Navy: the ship, then in Malta, retained its name but its initials 'H.M.S.' were changed to 'O.R.P.' ('Okret Rzeczypospolitej Polskiej'—Ship of the Polish Republic).

A new navy was slowly built on this modest basis and Polish vessels validly participated in war operations in the Atlantic and Mediterranean.

The old uniforms and insignia continued to be worn in Britain; new ones were tailored locally and the first amendments to the dress regulations were published in 1941. By the Order No. 5 of 27 October, Paragraph 53, the rings of gold lace previously placed all around the cuffs were replaced by stripes on the outside of the cuffs and the rate insignia of the cadets were changed to stripes on the cuffs, which identified 1st, 2nd or 3rd Year Course.

In April 1942, the Warrant Officer's insignia was replaced by a gold lace stripe ¼ in (6.3 mm) in width, with curl, worn on both cuffs. The Petty Officer was allowed to wear the cap and uniform previously strictly reserved for the chief petty officers.

A new Polish naval service composed of women was organised in April 1943, on the basis of the British 'Wrens' and with similar uniforms.

In November 1943, the naval staff dealt with the chaplains: the new regulations specified that they should wear officers' uniforms without rank stripes, with the Roman Cross in gold on the collar and shoulder straps, and one or two stripes on the visor of the peaked cap, according to rank. Chaplains were identified by their clerical collar.

The officers of Commissariat were given white distinction cloth in March 1944 and, in November, the branches of Naval Aviation and Coastal Defence were formed within the Navy. The personnel of the latter wore khaki army uniforms with a blue beret, blue shoulder straps with foul anchor, naval cap badges and army pattern rank insignia but in gold. The Coastal Defence was subdivided into three branches: Line, Technical and administration. All wore blue collar patches in two shapes: for officers' service dress and ratings' battledress, as the patches had to match the different shapes of the collar. The collar patches had coloured piping at the top, as follows:

Branch	**Colour**
Line	White
Technical	Dark green
Administration	Brown

The very last amendments to the dress regulations were published in September 1945 and dealt with the Coastal Defence and Naval Aviation. The officers of the latter were ordered to wear an 'L' ('Lotnictwo') inside the curl of their rank stripes.

Netherlands

Only since 1815, when the Netherlands became a kingdom, can one speak of the Royal Netherlands Navy, although the history of the Dutch Navy goes back to the early thirteenth century. During the latter part of the sixteenth and the beginning of the seventeenth century, sea battles took place between Dutch and Spanish fleets. Some famous battles were those of Zuider Zee (1573), the Armada (1588), Sluys (1603), Gibraltar (1607), the Slaak (1631) and the Downs (1639).

After the Eighty Years' War was concluded by the Treaty of Westphalia, by which the independence of the Republic of the United Provinces was recognised, the Dutch neglected their navy, with the result that, during the First Anglo–Dutch War, the latter were beaten and the Low Countries had to concur with the Treaty of Westminster, which proved inconclusive.

In the second half of the seventeenth century Dutch naval power was restored in all waters which were important to commerce; in the Baltic and its approaches, in the North Sea, in the Mediterranean and in the Caribbean, Dutch ships-of-war came into action when commercial interests had to be defended. Some famous battles were the Four Days' Battle (1666), Chatham (1667), Sole Bay (1672), Schooneveld (1673), Texel (1673), Oland (1676), Beachy Head (1690) and La Hogue (1692).

Great admirals like Tromp, De Ruyter, Kortenaer, Banckert, Evertsen and many others led their fleets to victory.

The eighteenth century saw the decline of Dutch sea power until 1780 when the Fourth Anglo-Dutch war broke out. During this war, which lasted four years, the battle of Doggerbank (1781) was fought.

In 1795, the Batavian Republic was proclaimed and, once again, Dutch and English ships met at sea and, at Camperdown (1797), one of the bloodiest naval battles was fought. In 1806 the Republic became the Kingdom of Holland with the brother of Napoleon, Louis, as king. In 1810 this kingdom was incorporated into the French Empire and, after the defeat of Napoleon, the Netherlands became a kingdom, in 1815.

During the nineteenth century and the beginning of the twentieth the Royal Netherlands Navy was mainly employed in the pacification of the Dutch colonies in the Far East and the suppression of piracy. During World War 1, its main task was the maintenance of neutrality and it was not until the outbreak of World War 2 that the Royal Netherlands Navy was again involved in combat, and suffered severe losses.

Plate 63. Cap and Rank Insignia

The officers of the various corps of the Royal Netherlands Navy were identified by badges rather than by corps colours. The cap badge of all except chaplains consisted of a wreath of twelve oak leaves and acorns ensigned by the crown, with the corps' emblem in the centre: the chaplains' badge had no crown and its wreath had eight oak leaves only. All wreaths had six acorns.

The following were the corps, their emblems and type of embroidery:

Corps	Emblem	Embroidery
Line	Foul anchor	Gold
Administration	Foul anchor	Silver
Engineering	Torch above crossed arrows	Gold
Medical	Aesculapius staff	Gold
Aviation	Aircraft engine above propeller	Gold
Chaplains	Roman Cross	Gold

Flag officers wore peaked caps with two rows of oak leaves and acorns on the visor, the captain and commander had one row only along the edge. All the other officers, the chaplains, warrant and petty officers had plain black leather visors.

The Warrant Officer and Petty Officer wore the crown and anchor on the cap, in silver for Yeomen and gold for all others; musicians had the lyre below the crown, the whole in gold.

Officers and warrant officers displayed rank insignia on the cuffs or on the shoulder straps, according to uniform. The flag officers displayed one large and one medium stripe of gold lace, the latter with the curl, and their individual rank was identified by small 6-pointed silver stars placed as shown in the illustrations.

Plate 64. Rank Insignia and Collar Badges

Administrative officers wore silver lace stripes, all the others gold stripes. Chaplains were restricted to one rank only ('Vloot Geestelijke') with two gold stripes and a separate silver one above; they did not have a curl but, contrary to all the other officers, they wore their badge on the shoulder straps.

The officers of the Special Service ('Officieren voor Speciale Diensten') had the initials 'SD' in the curl and could rank up to Captain only; they were reserve officers who were enlisted for special duties.

The collar badges worn on the blue jacket were the same as the corps emblem of the cap badges, except for the chaplains who wore the usual cross surrounded by a wreath with four oak leaves and two acorns, the same badge as on the shoulder straps.

The personnel serving in line and aviation, and the chaplains, had the same gold buttons with crown above the anchor; administration had the same buttons but made of silver; engineers had the crowned anchor superimposed upon crossed torch and arrow and medical personnel's buttons displayed the crown above the Aesculapius staff surrounded by an oak wreath. The buttons of the latter two were made of gold, in accordance with the general rules.

The Warrant Officer was identified by a narrow stripe with curl worn on the cuffs or shoulder straps, of gold or silver as usual.

Plate 65. Ratings' Insignia

The three ratings of the Royal Netherlands Navy wore chevrons on the cuffs of the blue jacket, the Chief Petty Officer and Petty Officer had two gold chevrons and one respectively; the Leading Seaman wore two yellow chevrons, or white ones in the case of a Yeoman Leading Seaman, on the cuffs of the overcoat.

The Chief and Petty Officer wore special patches with small chevrons, as above, on the collar of the white and khaki tropical tunic, while the Leading Seaman had one inverted 'V' chevron on the upper sleeves of the jumper or tropical uniform.

Warrant Officers' and Petty Officers' Speciality Badges

The warrant and petty officers wore speciality insignia of gold on the left sleeve of the blue uniform.

The Warrant Officer of most specialities was called 'Opper' plus his speciality title, but the Warrant Officers' Machinist was known as 'Adjudant-onderofficier-machinist' and a pilot as 'Adjudant-onderofficier-vlieger'.

The Chief Petty Officer Boatswain's title was 'Schipper' and all the others were known by their speciality title preceded by the word 'Majoor'.

The Petty Officer Boatswain was called 'Bootsman'; the others had their speciality title preceded by 'Sergeant.'

All the badges illustrated were made of gold wire, except the crown of the Yeoman which was made of silver.

The traditional Dutch cap tally displayed the title 'Royal Navy' in gothic script and was later replaced by another one, illustrated, with the title in block letters, yellow on black silk.

Plate 66. Speciality and Trade Badges

Speciality badges, in gold for leading seamen and red for seamen, were worn on the left upper sleeve of the blue uniform but not on tropical uniform; on the jumper of the white summer uniform no badges, except the chevron, were worn by leading seamen.

Bar exceptions, gold badges were used by the Leading Seaman and Seaman 1st Class, red ones by Seaman 2nd Class and apprentices.

Examples of speciality badges have been illustrated but there were more: there were four variations of badges for Torpedoman, Aviation Repairman, Electrician and Fire Controlman, a gold badge for Leading Seaman and Seaman 1st Class, a red badge with two small bars below for the 3rd Year Apprentice, with one bar for the 2nd Year Apprentice and the red badge without any bar for the 1st Year Apprentice. Carpenters wore a gold badge, a red one with bar and another without a bar.

The trade badge was worn on the right upper sleeve of the blue uniform. Beside those illustrated, red crossed flags were used by signallers, crossed flags and lightning by telegraphists, crossed guns by gunners and gold crossed guns were awarded to the Marksman Gunner. The last two rows of badges illustrated were trade badges; those above were speciality badges.

Finland

Many Finns served in the Swedish Navy during the period when Finland belonged to Sweden, from the twelfth century to 1809, and later in the Russian Navy. No less than three hundred became officers and seventy of them reached the rank of rear-admiral and above during the latter period.

After the Russo-Swedish War of 1808–09, Finland became part of the Russian Empire as an autonomous grand duchy, retaining its own laws and institutions, and even some national defence forces which included small naval units called Sea Equipage.

Finland became an independent republic on 6 December 1917 as a result of the Russian Revolution and, after the War of Independence fought by government troops against Russian and Finnish Reds, the Finnish Navy was established in the summer of 1918. The ships were those that the Russians had left behind and the officers were Finns who had served in the Russian Navy and some German naval experts.

In the 1920s, British naval experts were employed in reorganising and planning a new ship-building programme, which was carried out in the next decade.

During the Winter War (December 1939–March 1940) the Finnish Navy consisted of the following units: the Helsinki Naval Base, the Turku Naval Base and the Coastal Fleet, but operations were restricted by the severe weather from the beginning of January onwards, when the whole Baltic Sea was frozen.

After the Germans had started Operation 'Barbarossa' Finland became involved in another war against the U.S.S.R., which ended with the Armistice of Moscow, in September 1944. The Peace Treaty was finally signed in Paris on 10 February 1947.

Plate 67. Cap and Rank Insignia

The first official naval uniforms were introduced in 1919 and followed the international naval pattern with some Russian and German features.

The executive officers' cap badge depicted the gold Finnish Lion on a round, protruding red enamel background, on a gold base. On the peaked cap (lippalakki') this badge was centred between two sprays of gold embroidered laurel leaves, below a gold anchor. The white-blue-white cockade, in brass and enamel, was used by cadets of the Reserve, warrant and petty officers, and also by officers, and a painted version of this badge was worn by seamen.

Two rows of gold oak leaves on the peaked cap's visor identified flag officers and one row senior officers, from the rank of Kommodori to Komentajakapteeni.

The Finnish Lion was always worn in conjunction with the rank stripes by all executive officers, usually above the stripes but, in the case of the flag officers' shoulder straps, it was worn superimposed upon the wide stripe, as illustrated. The stripes were made of gold lace, 1 of 1⅝ in (40 mm) in width for flag officers, $\frac{19}{32}$ in (15 mm) and $\frac{7}{32}$ in (5 mm) the narrower stripes.

Shoulder straps were used on the white uniform, overcoat and fur coat while, on all other uniforms, rank insignia was displayed on the cuffs.

Plate 68. Cap and Rank Insignia

Non-executive officers wore the same uniform as executive officers but had an additional stripe, or stripes of distinction cloth with the rows of gold lace on the cuffs and shoulder straps. The distinction cloth filled the interval, or intervals between two or more stripes or it was placed below a single stripe. The branches were identified as follows:

Branch	**Distinction Cloth**
Executive Officers	None
Engineer Officers	Violet
Medical Officers	Red
Musicians	Blue

The officers of the Reserve wore special stripes, of gold lace but adapted to a zigzag pattern, until the summer of 1940 when this distinction was abolished.

Only one rank of Chaplain existed and was identified by a cross above a large stripe placed on the cuffs and shoulder straps.

Specialist officers were distinguished by silver insignia and by a 6-pointed star worn in conjunction with their rank stripes, instead of the Finnish Lion. They had silver embroidered cap badges, silver stripes, silver shoulder tabs, buttons, etc.

The shoulder tabs or epaulettes, according to order of dress, were worn on the frock coat in use before the war. The dress belt is another item that was abolished during the war: the flag officers' belt was made of gold lace and carried a design of oak leaves and acorns, the officers' belt had horizontal alternate gold and blue stripes and the warrant officers had a plain cloth belt. However, the buckle and fittings could be attached to a leather belt as well, which was worn on service dress in lieu of a Sam Browne belt.

Plate 69. Cadets' Cap and Rank Insignia

The cadets of the regular navy wore, on the peaked cap, the officers' Finnish Lion above four gold embroidered laurel leaves, the whole badge edged by a thin blue cord. Basically they wore officers' uniforms while the cadets of the Reserve had seamen's uniforms and therefore seamen's head-dress, with their own cap tally and petty officers' cockade made of metal and enamel.

The former had special shoulder straps for full dress. These straps had rounded inner ends, were edged with gold lace and carried the Naval Academy's badge on the outer ends and an anchor or crossed cannons in the centre, which identified navy or coast artillery branch, respectively.

The anchor or the crossed cannons devices were also worn on the left upper sleeve, together with chevrons; inverted 'V' chevrons on the top to identify progress of training and 'V' chevrons below that showed the cadet's rank, as they attained petty officers' rank while at the Academy.

Reserve officer cadets were eligible to two ranks only, Candidate and Cadet, which were identified by two, or one, upper chevrons worn above the 'RUK' badge ('Reserviupseerikoula'—Reserve Officers' School).

Warrant Officers' Rank Insignia

The warrant officers wore officers' uniforms with badges of their own pattern. They were divided into three classes and displayed rank insignia in the form of inverted 'V' chevrons, $\frac{9}{32}$ in (7 mm) in width, on both cuffs of the jacket. Above the apex of the chevrons they had the speciality badge, embroidered in gold. Speciality badges were also worn on the shoulder straps, which were of officers' pattern but made of plain cloth.

All these badges have been illustrated in this and the following plate; the 'Master' rank title was used by the warrant officers while the plain title of speciality refers to the ratings.

Plate 70. Warrant Officers' and Petty Officers' Insignia

The warrant officers' cap badge consisted of the white-blue-white enamelled cockade centred between a gold embroidered anchor and a four-leaf laurel spray, the whole edged by a blue cord.

The naval petty officers had the same cockade below a gold metal anchor, placed on an oval background edged by a gold cord. The specialist petty officers wore only a white metal anchor surrounded by a silver cord.

Petty Officers' Rate Insignia

The petty officers wore gold chevrons (silver for specialists) on the left upper sleeve and, except for the top and bottom ranks, they had army titles divided into three grades: Senior Sergeant, Sergeant and Junior Sergeant. The boatswains had wide chevrons, while the other ratings had narrow ones, $\frac{9}{32}$ in (7 mm) in width, with gold speciality badges above them.

There were three classes of seamen identified by blue anchors and blue bars. The petty officer candidate wore a plain white bar.

Conscripted seamen were also eligible for ratings but their badges were red: initially one horizontal red bar, two red bars and, later, an individual could attain one or two red chevrons and speciality badges made of red felt.

All seamen and conscripted petty officers wore the sailor's hat with silk tally and a tin badge painted white and blue.